Please return/renew this item by the last
date shown. Books may also be renewed
by phone or Internet.

 www.rbwm.gov.uk/web/libraries.htm

☎ 01628 796969 (library hours)

☎ 0303 123 0035 (24 hours)

The Royal Borough
Windsor &
Maidenhead

POWER PULSES

Tami Hardeman

CONTENTS

INTRODUCTION TO PULSES

WHAT ARE PULSES?

From the Latin word *puls*, meaning porridge or thick soup, pulses are the dried, edible seeds of a legume plant. Nutritious and sustainable, they are an integral part of many cuisines and an easy way to put protein on your plate.

A KITCHEN STAPLE

Tasty and versatile, pulses are a class of legume. Unlike other legume pods that are fresh-harvested or fatty (such as fresh beans, fresh peas, peanuts, and soya beans), pulses are harvested after they've dried within the pod. The dehydrated seeds are an inexpensive protein source that you can store for years, making them a store cupboard staple. Once cooked, pulses can be enjoyed in a host of applications, from sweet to savoury. Whether they are braised, roasted, sprouted, or puréed, pulses are embraced by vegetarians, vegans, and omnivores alike for their nutrition, convenience, and flavour.

Legumes are any plant whose seed is enclosed within a pod

Pulses are legume seeds that are harvested when they're dry

HOW THEY'RE GROWN AND HARVESTED

Unlike many legumes, pulses are dry-harvested once fully mature. Home cooks then rehydrate the seeds by soaking them in liquid so they're suitable for cooking.

1
Farmers choose and plant their seeds in spring in the northern hemisphere and late autumn in the southern hemisphere. Wet weather is best for planting.

2
Farmers may roll crop beds flat after planting to improve harvest rates. Low-hanging pods are less likely to break when they're cleanly separated from the soil.

3
The pods mature through the next season. Dry weather is ideal for harvesting, so some farmers apply chemicals to aid drying, especially during cold, wet seasons.

ALL SHAPES & SIZES

From tiny beluga lentils to giant broad beans, pulses come in a vast array of sizes, colours, and textures. They are often grouped into four categories – dry beans, dry peas, lentils, and chickpeas – all of which are easy to prepare and packed with fibre and protein.

DRY BEANS

The varieties of dry beans are virtually boundless, but each type is nutritionally dense and deliciously versatile. Cook your beans in batches, then experiment with their unique flavours and textures by incorporating them into a variety of different dishes.

DRY PEAS

Unlike fresh peas, which are often eaten directly from the pod, dry peas are harvested and shelled once fully mature. Available both split and whole, these pulses have a slightly sweet, earthy flavour and a thick, creamy texture that makes them ideal for soups.

LENTILS

Available in a range of colours and sizes, these tiny lens-shaped seeds are sold both split and whole. They don't require soaking, so they're quick to cook and hold their shape well. The flavour and texture of lentils are especially suited to soups, salads, and braised dishes.

CHICKPEAS

This pulse variety has a distinct hazelnut-like shape. Often found in Indian and Mediterranean cuisines, these plump, firm seeds have a nutty flavour and starchy, creamy texture that is perfect for roasting or blending into dips.

4
Once the pods and seeds have dried, pulses are ready to harvest. If they are harvested too early, then the seeds are too moist for storage.

5
At harvest time, the pods are plucked from the plants. The dry seeds are separated from the pods, and the pods are discarded.

6
The seeds are processed to ensure quality. Your pulses are cleaned, sorted, split, and milled before finding their way to shop shelves and your table.

Kitchen-ready pulses

WHY EAT PULSES?

Pulses not only taste delicious, they're also a great choice for both your body and the environment. These humble seeds boast substantial health benefits, and they are one of the most economical and sustainable sources of food.

THEY'RE GOOD FOR YOU

High in essential vitamins and minerals but low in fat, pulses are widely considered to be a superfood that can fight disease and contribute to a long, healthy life. Pulses are particularly good sources of fibre and protein, a pairing that provides sustained energy but keeps cholesterol levels low.

Beans, chickpeas, peas, and lentils contain between 20 and 25 per cent protein by weight, much more than many other plant-based protein sources, such as spinach and quinoa. This makes them an attractive alternative to meat-based proteins, particularly for vegans and vegetarians.

Pulses are also rich in key minerals like iron, potassium, zinc, and manganese, all of which play important roles in maintaining health.

per serving **CHICKPEAS have 5X** more **IRON** than **SPINACH**

Health benefits

Preserve heart health
Cholesterol-free and low in fat, pulses reduce the risk of heart disease.

Boost energy
Pulses are rich in iron, which helps transport oxygen in your bloodstream, rejuvenating your cells and your body.

Build strong bones
Dense in manganese and other important nutrients, pulses promote healthy bone structure.

Maintain the gut
Pulses are fibre-packed and high in prebiotics, your body's natural digestive regulators.

Improve brain function
High in folic acid, pulses can improve mental and emotional health.

Aid weight loss
Pulses contain amino acids that boost metabolism, as well as soluble fibre to make you feel fuller for longer.

Control diabetes
Complex carbohydrates and a low Glycaemic Index provide steady glucose release to regulate insulin in the blood.

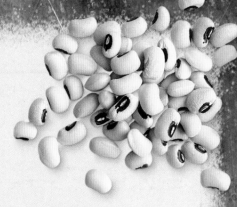

THEY'RE GOOD FOR THE PLANET

Not just good for your body, pulses are good for everybody. Kilogram for kilogram, they can feed more people than meat and require just a fraction of the resources required to raise livestock. Growing pulses also enriches the soil, improving crop yield.

Greater water efficiency

Pulse crops such as lentils and chickpeas are well adapted to semi-arid climates and are more drought-tolerant than other crops, so they require less water than other plants and livestock. They also use water differently from other crops, drawing from the shallow depth of the soil and leaving the deeper-down water in place for the next year's growth.

Water used to produce one kilogram

Growing pulses is significantly more sustainable for the environment than rearing livestock. It takes 43 times more water to produce 1kg of beef than 1kg of pulses.

pulses	soya beans	chicken	pork	beef
74 litres	371 litres	800 litres	1,298 litres	3,195 litres

Reduced carbon footprint

It takes energy to produce food, and that energy generates greenhouse gas emissions. But pulses are more eco-friendly than other foods because they require no nitrogen fertilizer. Nitrogen fertilizer uses energy-intensive production processes and emits nitrous oxide, which has nearly 300 times the global warming potential of carbon dioxide.

The water savings of growing **165 kg** OF PULSES instead of beef would fill an OLYMPIC SIZE POOL

Increased food security

For many people, regular access to meat, dairy, and fish can be cost prohibitive. Pulses provide a safe and nutritious food at a low cost, and their long shelf life means they can be stored for months without losing nutritional value, reducing food waste.

Especially in developing countries, pulses help lift farmers out of rural poverty. Pulses can command prices two to three times higher than cereal crops, and their processing provides local job opportunities.

Higher crop yields

Farmers all around the world know how important pulses are to their sustainable farming systems. Unlike most crops, pulses extract nitrogen from the air around them and fix it to the soil, leaving behind nitrogen-rich residues and other compounds that help fight disease and insects. This enriches the soil, making it possible for the next crop in rotation to produce higher yields.

LENTILS

Lentil cultivation dates back to 7000 BCE, making it one of the world's oldest crops. Now they're grown and eaten on nearly every continent. They don't require pre-soaking, so they're an easy protein-packed supplement for plant-based diets.

GREEN LENTIL ▶

Also called Puy lentil, Lentilles du Puy, and French green lentil

The green lentil has a rich, deep flavour and holds its shape well after cooking. Use it in salads, stews, and casseroles to accentuate its firm texture.

Nutrition per 100g, cooked

Calories 115 **Protein** 9g
Carbohydrates 20g **Fibre** 8g

Good source of iron

Excellent source of fibre

◀ BROWN LENTIL

Varieties include Spanish pardina, German brown, Indian brown, and brewer lentil

The most common type of lentil, this ranges from a light khaki colour to a deep, ruddy brown. It has a creamy, slightly nutty taste that works in a variety of cuisines. Moderately firm, it can either hold its shape in soups and casseroles or mash easily for burgers and rissoles.

Nutrition per 100g, cooked

Calories 115 **Protein** 9g
Carbohydrates 20g **Fibre** 8g

Good source of potassium and vitamin B6

Excellent source of folate

◄ BELUGA LENTIL

Also called black lentil and petite beluga lentil

The shiny and small black pulse is named after the caviar it resembles. The beluga lentil is mild in flavour and holds its shape when cooked, making it a great ingredient for salads, pilafs, and stuffings.

Nutrition per 100g, cooked

Calories 122 **Protein** 9g
Carbohydrates 22g **Fibre** 11g

Good source of amino acids

Excellent source of protein

◄ YELLOW LENTIL

Also called golden lentil, toor dal, arhar dal, and tan lentils

Similar to red lentils, the yellow lentil is mild, sweet, and faintly nutty. It disintegrates quickly during cooking, which works well in spreads and soups. You'll often find yellow lentils in Indian dishes such as curries and dal.

Nutrition per 100g, cooked

Calories 115 **Protein** 9g
Carbohydrates 20g **Fibre** 8g

Good source of potassium

Excellent source of manganese

◄ RED LENTIL

Also called petite red lentil, crimson lentil, and red chief

Mild and slightly sweet, this lentil is pinkish-orange and sold both whole and split. Since it's very small, it breaks down quickly once cooked and is ideal for soups and dips. You can even use red lentils as a thickening agent for gravies and stews.

Nutrition per 100g, cooked

Calories 115 **Protein** 9g
Carbohydrates 20g **Fibre** 8g

Good source of slow-digesting carbohydrates and fibre

Excellent source of zinc and iron

175g LENTILS	VS.	175g minced BEEF
calories	192	VS.	361
sat. fat	0g	VS.	10g
cholesterol	0mg	VS.	114mg
protein	18g	VS.	31g

BEANS

From the common to the exotic, there are many types of dried beans to explore and enjoy. Seek out unfamiliar varieties to experience the full range of flavours and textures.

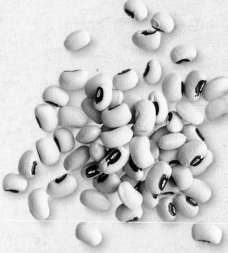

HARICOT BEAN ▶

Also called navy bean, pea bean, and white pea bean

Small and creamy, the haricot bean is oval shaped and slightly flattened. It's excellent for baked beans, soups, dips, and spreads. In addition to lots of healthy protein, the haricot is full of dietary fibre that helps stabilize blood sugar.

Nutrition per 100g, cooked

Calories 112 **Protein** 6g
Carbohydrates 21g **Fibre** 9g

Good source of copper and iron

Excellent source of iron, folate, and manganese

BLACK-EYED BEAN ▲

Also called cowpea, California buckeye, and purple hull pea

Grown all over the world, the black-eyed bean usually has a single, prominent spot before it's cooked. It appears in salads, rice dishes, and soups, and complements bold flavours.

Nutrition per 100g, cooked

Calories 109 **Protein** 7g
Carbohydrates 19g **Fibre** 7g

Good source of potassium

Excellent source of vitamin K

◀ ADZUKI BEAN

Also called azuki bean and aduki bean

Originating from Asia, this bean is small and burgundy. Its mild flavour lends itself to sweet preparations; red bean paste is common in many Asian desserts. Also use it as you would the black bean in soups and chillies.

Nutrition per 100g, cooked

Calories 144 **Protein** 9g
Carbohydrates 27g **Fibre** 8g

Good source of folate, vitamin B6, protein, and fibre

Excellent source of phosphorous, zinc, and potassium

◄ PINTO BEAN

Also called speckled bean and strawberry bean

Spanish for "painted", this medium-sized bean is speckled beige and red. When cooked, the specks disappear and the bean turns bright pink. It's perfect for refried beans and chilli.

Nutrition per 100g, cooked

Calories 162 **Protein** 10g
Carbohydrates 29g **Fibre** 10g

Good source of protein, phosphorous, and manganese

Excellent source of vitamin B1, vitamin B6, potassium, and iron

KIDNEY BEAN ▲

Also called red bean

This medium-sized red bean resembles a kidney in shape and colour. It is commonly found both dried and canned and is often used in soups and chillies. High in fibre and protein, kidney beans contribute to a healthy heart.

Nutrition per 100g, cooked

Calories 137 **Protein** 10g
Carbohydrates 24g **Fibre** 8g

Good source of iron and folate

Excellent source of calcium

◄ BUTTER BEAN

Also called lima bean and sieva bean

Dried butter beans are flat, kidney shaped, and white. The bean has a creamy texture, which makes it perfect for dips among other recipes. Despite its name and rich texture, the butter bean is a nearly fat-free source of protein and fibre.

Nutrition per 100g, cooked

Calories 138 **Protein** 9g
Carbohydrates 25g **Fibre** 9g

Good source of folate and magnesium

Excellent source of soluble fibre

◄ BLACK BEAN

Also called black turtle bean

Shiny and black, this bean earns its nickname "turtle" because of its smooth shell exterior. The black bean's meaty texture and mild taste makes it perfect for vegetarian recipes. It's commonly found in soups and served with rice in many cultures.

Nutrition per 100g, cooked

Calories 149 **Protein** 8g
Carbohydrates 28g **Fibre** 12g

Good source of calcium, iron, and zinc

Excellent source of phytonutrients

◄ CANNELLINI BEAN

Also called Great Northern bean and white bean

This medium-sized flat bean has a creamy, off-white colour. Its hearty texture makes it a natural addition to soups and stews, braised dishes, and casseroles. It's an especially good substitute for the similar haricot bean and an excellent source of protein and fibre.

Nutrition per 100g, cooked

Calories 154 **Protein** 10g
Carbohydrates 27g **Fibre** 7g

Good source of vitamin C and magnesium

Excellent source of phosphorous, iron, and potassium

CONTINUED ▶

◀ MUNG BEAN

Also called moong bean, moong dal, and green gram

This small green pulse is used in both sweet and savoury recipes. It is commonly found in Indian and Asian cooking but can also easily be sprouted. So-called beansprouts are usually sprouted mung beans.

Nutrition per 100g, cooked

Calories 125 **Protein** 8g
Carbohydrates 22g **Fibre** 9g

Good source of fibre and protein

Excellent source of folate, magnesium, and vitamin B1

◀ SCARLET RUNNER

Also called runner bean and multiflora bean

Originally from Mexico, the scarlet runner bean is one of the oldest cultivated foods in the Americas. The large bean is a striking purple and black colour and has a dense, meaty texture. It's best used in stews, casseroles, and chillies.

Nutrition per 100g, cooked

Calories 186 **Protein** 10g
Carbohydrates 41g **Fibre** 17g

Good source of vitamin B1, niacin, and potassium

Excellent source of calcium and fibre

FLAGEOLET ▲

Varieties include chevrier and Flambeau

From France, this small, pale mint-green and kidney-shaped bean is an exquisite treat. Simple preparations, herbs, and dressings highlight the firm and creamy texture and mild taste.

Nutrition per 100g, cooked

Calories 139 **Protein** 10g
Carbohydrates 25g **Fibre** 6g

Good source of vitamin C

Excellent source of fibre

BORLOTTI BEAN ▶

Also called cranberry bean, Roman bean, saluggia bean, and rosecoco bean

Tender, moist, and beautifully speckled when dry, the borlotti bean turns brown when cooked. It is plump, bittersweet, and excellent for vegetable stews, casseroles, and salads.

Nutrition per 100g, cooked

Calories 136 **Protein** 9g
Carbohydrates 24g **Fibre** 10g

Good source of phosphorous

Excellent source of iron

MOTH BEAN ◄

Also called moath bean, moat bean, matki, mat bean, and Turkish gram

Cultivated in many parts of the world, from India to Italy, the moth bean is a small, light brown cylindrical pulse with a nutty flavour. Its flavour profile complements aromatic spices, coconut, and foods with a touch of sweetness.

Nutrition per 100g, cooked

Calories 81 **Protein** 5g
Carbohydrates 14g **Fibre** 6g

Good source of iron and magnesium

Excellent source of folate

BROAD BEAN ▲

Also called faba bean, fava bean

The long-cultivated broad bean is meaty, earthy, buttery, and bold. After soaking, most cooks prefer to pop each bean out of its skin before cooking. Though large, it disintegrates quickly, making it a great candidate to purée or mash.

Nutrition per 100g, cooked

Calories 110 **Protein** 8g
Carbohydrates 20g **Fibre** 5g

Good source of phosphorous, copper, and manganese

Excellent source of folate

BLACK LENTIL ▲

Also called vinga mungo, black gram, black urad dal, and mungo bean

Most often used in Indian cooking, the black lentil is actually a bean. The small, black cylindrical pulse has a creamy white interior. Its deep, earthy flavour makes it a perfect match for curries, stews, and other boldly flavoured dishes.

Nutrition per 100g, cooked

Calories 127 **Protein** 10g
Carbohydrates 22g **Fibre** 9g

Good source of magnesium

Excellent source of iron, folic acid, and calcium

HEIRLOOM BEANS

Untouched by genetic science, there are endless varieties of heirloom beans, each with a unique look and depth of flavour. They are cultivated in a single setting for generations, never mass-produced, so the genetic pureness produces the same seed with each generation of planting. Heirlooms are not usually on the shelves of ordinary stores, but when you do find them, they are a culinary delight.

Orca bean

CHICKPEAS

There are two main types of chickpeas – desi and kabuli. The desi is small and dark; the more common kabuli is larger and paler, and usually just labelled "chickpea".

PEAS

Unlike peanuts and fresh peas, dry peas are low in fat and harvested dry. Pigeon peas and split peas are the most common, but you can also find green and yellow peas in whole form.

◄ PIGEON PEA

Also called split toor dal

Nutty and crisp, the pigeon pea is a key food source around the world – hearty, drought resistant, and cultivated for over 3,000 years. The small, glossy brown pea is often served alongside rice for a complete meal.

Nutrition per 100g, cooked

Calories 171 **Protein** 9g
Carbohydrates 30g
Fibre 9g

Good source of folate

Excellent source of magnesium

CHICKPEA ▲

Also called garbanzo bean, gram, Bengal gram, chana dal, kabuli

This domesticated chickpea dates back to mesolithic cultures. Not actually a true pea, it has a nutty flavour and creamy texture. Its soft, starchy quality makes it a versatile ingredient for dips, salads, spreads, and curries.

Nutrition per 100g, cooked

Calories 157 **Protein** 9g
Carbohydrates 26g **Fibre** 7g

Good source of antioxidants

Excellent source of fibre

SPLIT PEA ►

Varieties include green split pea and yellow split pea

The split pea is harvested whole then split in half. It is similar in taste and texture to lentils but rounder in shape and brighter in colour. It's best known for making soups and Indian dal, but also works well in dips and spreads.

Nutrition per 100g, cooked

Calories 116 **Protein** 8g
Carbohydrates 20g **Fibre** 8g

Good source of vitamin A

Excellent source of low-fat protein

PULSE FLOURS

Almost any pulse can be ground into a flour, but white beans, chickpeas, and black beans are the most common. They don't contain gluten, so they're an excellent addition to restricted diets.

Pulse flours taste different from traditional wheat flour, each with a unique flavour profile. Use them for baking, soups, dips, and bread, as well as for binding and thickening. Substituting some or all of the wheat flour in recipes with a pulse flour adds extra nutrition to your cooking. When used for baking, you'll need to combine pulse flours with another gluten-free or traditional wheat flour to help mixtures rise.

◀ WHITE BEAN FLOUR

This flour is extremely mild. When combined with stabilizers such as Xanthan gum or potato starch, white bean flour is an excellent substitute in gluten-free baking. Its creamy texture makes it a natural addition to soups, sauces, and gravies.

Nutrition per 100g

Calories 155 **Protein** 10g
Carbohydrates 28g **Fibre** 11g

Good source of folate and manganese

Excellent source of phosphorous

▲ CHICKPEA FLOUR

This is one of the most versatile pulse flours. It's creamy, sweet, and slightly nutty, making it a great addition to baked goods and pizza dough. Use it in recipes that contain bold flavours, such as pumpkin bread or Middle Eastern dishes.

Nutrition per 100g

Calories 211 **Protein** 11g
Carbohydrates 26g **Fibre** 7g

Good source of iron

Excellent source of dietary fibre

BLACK BEAN FLOUR ▶

Ground from black turtle beans, black bean flour has a deep, rich, earthy flavour. It's sometimes simply mixed with water and served as a dip, but it can also be used a thickener or filling in Mexican recipes.

Nutrition per 100g

Calories 171 **Protein** 11g
Carbohydrates 31g **Fibre** 7g

Good source of dietary fibre

Excellent source of low-fat protein

HOW TO COOK PULSES

Cooking dried pulses rewards you with depth of flavour and control of variables such as consistency and salt levels. Simmering on the hob is the most common method, but you can also use a slow cooker or pressure cooker.

1 PREPARE

Sort the pulses on a baking tray, removing broken and irregular pieces as well as foreign objects, such as small stones. Then remove any dirt and grit by rinsing the pulses in a fine sieve.

2 SOAK

Place the pulses in a large bowl and cover with cool water to about 5cm (2in) above the level of the pulses. Most should soak for 8 hours or overnight.

3 DRAIN & RINSE

Drain and rinse the pulses again in a fine sieve under cool water, to wash away impurities or toxins released by soaking.

4 COOK

Transfer to a stock pot. Cover with water to at least 5cm (2in) above the level of the pulses. Bring to the boil, reduce to a simmer and cook according to the pulse's cooking time (see page 23). Periodically skim off any foam that develops on the surface.

5 CHECK

For a perfectly cooked batch, check your pulses within the suggested cooking time range by pinching and tasting a few from the pot.

Perfect
A perfectly cooked, tender pulse will yield easily when pinched and is soft throughout while maintaining its shape.

Undercooked
An undercooked pulse is too firm and will not give when pinched, indicating that it needs more cooking time.

Overcooked
An overcooked pulse is mushy and loses its shape, but you can still salvage the batch for dips, spreads, and purées.

Adding flavour

For a robust flavour, use stock instead of water, and add bay leaves, onions, garlic, and other aromatics to the cooking liquid. However, don't add salt until the last half hour of cooking. Salt added too early can toughen the skins and prolong cooking time.

Batch cooking & freezing

Most cooked pulse varieties freeze well, making it easy to keep them on hand. Let cooked pulses dry and cool completely, then portion into airtight plastic freezer bags. They will keep safely in the fridge for up to 3 days or in the freezer for several months without losing nutritional value.

Using canned beans

Canned beans can be used in place of home-cooked beans in any recipe. Make sure you thoroughly rinse them first, because the canning liquid can nearly double the salt content. A 400g (14oz) can contains about 230–250g (8½–9oz) drained beans.

Recipes work equally well with home-cooked or canned pulses.

SPROUTING

Sprouted pulses are fresh, crisp, and bursting with nutrients. Before you start, make sure you select a pulse variety that is suitable for sprouting.

1 In a large jar, generously cover the pulses with water. Cover the jar with cheesecloth and secure. Soak in a cool, dark place for 8 hours or overnight.

2 Drain the jar. Run fresh water through to rinse the pulses once or twice. Then tip the jar on its side and let the water drain completely.

3 Return to the storage space to allow the pulses to sprout. About every 12 hours, repeat step 2, then return to the storage space, leaving the jar lying tipped up on its side if preferred.

4 When the sprouts reach the desired length, remove from the jar and dry. Most varieties require 2–4 days to reach an average length. Store in an airtight bag or container in the fridge.

PERFECTLY PREPARED

Some pulses require soaking and a long simmer time, others cook quickly, and many are perfect for sprouting, or swapping in and out of your favourite recipes.

		Soaking time	On the hob simmer time	Pressure cooker time (on high)	Slow cooker time (on low)	Suitable for sprouting	Good substitutes
PEAS	Pigeon pea	8 hrs–overnight	45 mins–1 hr	6–9 mins	2–3 hrs	✸	Black-eyed bean
	Split pea	Not required	30 mins	1 min	6–8 hrs		Green lentil
LENTILS	Beluga lentil	Not required	25 mins	1 min	6–7 hrs	✸	Brown lentil, green lentil
	Brown lentil	Not required	20–25 mins	1 min	6–7 hrs	✸	Beluga lentil, green lentil
	Green lentil	Not required	20–25 mins	1 min	6–7 hrs	✸	Beluga lentil, brown lentil
	Red lentil	Not required	15–20 mins	1 min	6–7 hrs	✸	Yellow lentil
	Yellow lentil	Not required	15–20 mins	1 min	6–7 hrs	✸	Red lentil
BEANS	Adzuki bean	1–2 hrs	45 mins–1 hr	5–9 mins	6–8 hrs	✸	Mung bean
	Black bean	8 hrs–overnight	45 mins–1 hr	9–11 mins	6–8 hrs		Borlotti bean, pinto bean, haricot bean
	Black-eyed bean	8 hrs–overnight	1 hr	3–5 mins	6–8 hrs	✸	Pigeon pea
	Black lentil	8 hrs–overnight	30 mins	7 mins	6–8 hrs		Moth bean
	Borlotti bean	8 hrs–overnight	1 hr–1 hr 30 mins	7–10 mins	6–7 hrs		Cannellini bean, pinto bean
	Broad bean	8 hrs–overnight	1–2 hrs	10–12 mins	3–4 hrs	✸	Yellow split pea
	Chickpea	8 hrs–overnight	1 hr–1 hr 30 mins	10–12 mins	6–8 hrs		Cannellini bean
	Flageolet	8 hrs–overnight	1 hr–1 hr 30 mins	6–8 mins	6–7 hrs		Cannellini bean, haricot bean
	Cannellini bean	8 hrs–overnight	1 hr	8–12 mins	6–8 hrs		Haricot bean
	Kidney bean	8 hrs–overnight	1 hr–1 hr 30 mins	6–8 mins	6–7 hrs		Cannellini bean
	Butter bean	8 hrs–overnight	1 hr	4–7 mins	6–7 hrs		Haricot bean
	Moth bean	8 hrs–overnight	20–25 mins	5–6 mins	4–6 hrs	✸	Black lentil, beluga lentil
	Mung bean	Not required	30–45 mins	5–9 mins	6–8 hrs	✸	Adzuki bean
	Haricot bean	8 hrs–overnight	1 hr–1 hr 30 mins	6–8 mins	6–7 hrs		Cannellini bean
	Pinto bean	8 hrs–overnight	1 hr–1 hr 15 mins	4–6 mins	6–7 hrs		Kidney bean, borlotti bean
	Scarlet runner	8 hrs–overnight	1 hr 30 mins	5–8 mins	5–7 hrs		Kidney bean

BREAKFAST & BRUNCH

CURRIED MUNG BEAN AVOCADO TOAST

Sprouts and mung beans elevate avocado toast to the next level of tasty. The hint of curry flavour adds extra depth to the creamy, smooth avocado.

MAKES 3 · PREP 10 MINS · COOK 4 MINS

3 slices of sourdough or wholewheat bread

1 ripe avocado

175g (6oz) cooked mung beans

½ tsp curry powder

pinch of turmeric

salt and freshly ground black pepper

45g (1½oz) sprouted mung beans (beansprouts)

3 tbsp chopped chives

1 In a frying pan over a medium-low heat, toast the bread for 2 minutes on each side, or until brown and crisp. Remove from the frying pan and let cool slightly.

2 Cut the avocado in half and remove the pit. Scoop the flesh from one half and add to a medium mixing bowl. Mash the avocado half with a potato masher.

3 Stir in the mung beans, curry powder, and turmeric. Season with salt and pepper to taste. Spread the avocado mixture evenly over the slices of toast.

4 Remove the flesh from the remaining avocado half and slice thinly. Arrange equal amounts on each slice of toast.

5 Place on serving plates and sprinkle with the beansprouts and chives. Serve immediately.

Nutrition per toast

Calories	330
Total Fat	9g
Saturated Fat	1.5g
Cholesterol	0mg
Sodium	340mg
Total Carbohydrate	53g
Dietary Fibre	9g
Sugars	4g
Protein	14g

●Make it with meat

Crumble 2 rashers of cooked crispy bacon into the avocado–mung bean mixture.

LENTIL CREAM CHEESE TARTINES

Flavoured cream cheese is very easy to make at home. Adding lentils, chives, and lemon zest provides texture and some extra protein to this simple breakfast dish.

MAKES 6 · PREP 5 MINS · COOK 25 MINS

6 slices wholewheat bread

225g (8oz) cream cheese, softened

100g (3½oz) cooked brown lentils

2 tbsp chopped chives

zest of 1 lemon

salt and freshly ground black pepper

3 tsp olive oil

6 large eggs

115g (4oz) watercress

1 Preheat the oven to 150°C (300°F). Arrange the slices of bread on a baking sheet. Toast for 5 minutes, turn over, and toast for another 5 minutes until crisp and golden.

2 Meanwhile, to make the cream cheese spread, in a food processor blend the cream cheese, lentils, chives, and lemon zest until thoroughly combined. Season with salt and pepper to taste. Spread the mixture evenly over the slices of toast.

3 In a non-stick frying pan, heat 1 teaspoon of oil over a medium-low heat until shimmering. Crack 2 eggs into the frying pan and cook for 2–3 minutes until the whites are set but the yolks are runny. Place each egg atop a slice of toast then repeat with the remaining 4 eggs. Top each tartine with watercress and serve immediately.

Nutrition per tartine

Calories	280
Total Fat	17g
Saturated Fat	8g
Cholesterol	40mg
Sodium	400mg
Total Carbohydrate	22g
Dietary Fibre	4g
Sugars	4g
Protein	13g

● Make it with meat

Top each tartine with 30g (1oz) thinly sliced smoked salmon.

ROASTED TOMATO & CHICKPEA FRITTATA

Frittatas are a wonderful way to feed a crowd for breakfast or brunch. Chickpeas add an unexpected twist and extra body to this morning classic.

SERVES 10 · PREP 15 MINS · COOK 30 MINS

450g (1lb) baby plum
 tomatoes

1 garlic clove, finely chopped

2 sprigs of thyme

1 tbsp olive oil

10 large eggs

2 tbsp double cream

2 tsp chopped chives

salt and freshly ground black
 pepper

85g (3oz) baby spinach

350g (12oz) cooked chickpeas

1 Preheat the oven to 200°C (400°F). On a baking tray, toss the tomatoes, garlic, and thyme in the oil. Spread in an even layer and roast for 10 minutes. Discard the thyme. Let cool slightly.

2 Meanwhile, in a large mixing bowl whisk together the eggs, double cream, and chives. Season with salt and pepper.

3 Heat a 25cm (10-in) cast-iron or ovenproof frying pan over a medium heat. Transfer the tomatoes to the frying pan. Add the spinach and cook for 1–2 minutes until the spinach slightly wilts. Add the chickpeas and stir to combine. Spread the mixture evenly across the frying pan.

4 Pour the egg mixture over the tomatoes, spinach, and chickpeas. Cook uncovered for 2–3 minutes, until the edges of the egg begin to set. Transfer the frying pan to the oven and cook uncovered for an additional 8–10 minutes, until the edges are firm but the centre is still slightly springy. Serve immediately.

● **Make it
with meat**

Add 140g (5oz) finely diced cooked ham or chicken sausage to the frying pan with the chickpeas in step 3.

Nutrition per serving

Calories	130
Total Fat	8g
Saturated Fat	2.5g
Cholesterol	190mg
Sodium	360mg
Total Carbohydrate	7g
Dietary Fibre	2g
Sugars	2g
Protein	8g

Why not try…

For a creamy tang, sprinkle 115g (4oz) goat's cheese over the egg mixture before baking.

COCONUT, DATE & MOTH BEAN GRANOLA

Toasting the moth beans in this recipe makes them take on a dark colour and deep, caramelized taste. Their nutty flavour complements the sweetness of the dates and coconut.

SERVES 8 · PREP 20 MINS · COOK 50 MINS

400g (14oz) cooked moth beans

2 tbsp coconut oil

120ml (4fl oz) agave nectar

1 tsp vanilla extract

1 tsp cinnamon

100g (3½oz) roughly chopped almonds

75g (2½oz) roasted sunflower seeds

85g (3oz) pitted and chopped dates

30g (1oz) unsweetened coconut flakes

1 Preheat the oven to 180°C (325°F). Spread the moth beans on a light-coloured baking tray and let them dry for 5 minutes while measuring the remaining ingredients. Transfer the tray to the oven and toast the moth beans for 3–5 minutes until lightly crispy.

2 On the baking tray, toss the toasted moth beans with the coconut oil, agave, vanilla, and cinnamon. Arrange in a single layer, return to the oven, and bake for 6–8 minutes.

3 Remove the tray and stir in the almonds and sunflower seeds. Bake for another 20–30 minutes, stirring occasionally, until the mixture is toasted but not burnt.

4 Stir in the dates and coconut flakes. Return to the oven and bake for up to 5 more minutes, stirring as needed, until all the ingredients are toasted and crunchy. Remove from the oven and let sit for 10 minutes before serving. Store in an airtight container in the fridge for up to 3 days.

Nutrition per serving

Calories	230
Total Fat	14g
Saturated Fat	5g
Cholesterol	185mg
Sodium	0mg
Total Carbohydrate	24g
Dietary Fibre	6g
Sugars	13g
Protein	7g

Pulse exchange

Substitute an equal amount of **black lentils** or **beluga lentils** for the moth beans.

PEANUT & RED LENTIL GRANOLA BARS

These granola bars are a versatile, portable, and healthy home-made snack.

MAKES 10 · PREP 15 MINS, PLUS 3 HRS TO SET

125g (4½oz) cooked red lentils

140g (5oz) rolled oats

4 tbsp honey

30g (1oz) chia seeds

2 tbsp coconut oil

30g (1oz) roughly chopped almonds

⅓ tsp cinnamon

2 tsp vanilla extract

85g (3oz) smooth peanut butter

60g (2oz) plain chocolate chips, optional

1 Line a 20 x 20cm (8 x 8in) baking tin with baking parchment and set aside.

2 In a large mixing bowl, combine the lentils, oats, honey, chia seeds, coconut oil, almonds, cinnamon, vanilla, and peanut butter. Gently fold in the chocolate chips if using.

3 Transfer the mixture to the baking tin and spread evenly. Cover the tin with foil or cling film and refrigerate for 3 hours or overnight.

4 Use the parchment to remove the mixture from the tin. Cut the square in half then cut each half into 5 pieces, making 10 bars in total. Store in an airtight container in the fridge for up to 4 days.

● **Make it vegan**

Instead of honey, use the same amount of agave nectar.

Nutrition per bar

Calories	220
Total Fat	12g
Saturated Fat	4g
Cholesterol	0mg
Sodium	60mg
Total Carbohydrate	23g
Dietary Fibre	4g
Sugars	9g
Protein	7g

Why not try...
Add 30g (1oz) dried cranberries or chopped dates, instead of the chocolate chips.

CINNAMON RAISIN BREAKFAST QUINOA

Quinoa and lentils can be breakfast food too. With the warm flavours of vanilla, cinnamon, and almonds, this dish is as comforting as porridge but with more protein and fibre.

SERVES 6 · PREP 10 MINS · COOK 35 MINS

175g (6oz) quinoa

1 large vanilla pod

1 litre (1¾ pints) unsweetened almond milk

60ml (2fl oz) agave nectar or honey

1 cinnamon stick

¼ tsp ground nutmeg

100g (3½ oz) uncooked yellow lentils

115g (4oz) raisins

100g (3½ oz) chopped almonds

1 Place the quinoa in a fine sieve and rinse thoroughly. Let air dry slightly.

2 Cut the vanilla pod down the middle lengthways. Scrape out the seeds. Reserve both seeds and pod.

3 In a medium saucepan, combine the almond milk, agave, cinnamon stick, nutmeg, and vanilla seeds and pod. Gently bring to the boil. Add the quinoa and lentils. Cook, covered, for 20–25 minutes, until the lentils and quinoa are tender and most of the liquid is absorbed. Remove the vanilla pod and cinnamon stick.

4 To serve, divide among six bowls. Drizzle with additional almond milk if desired, then top each bowl with raisins and chopped almonds.

Pulse exchange
Instead of yellow lentils, use an equal amount of **red lentils.**

Nutrition per serving

Calories	410
Total Fat	13g
Saturated Fat	1g
Cholesterol	0mg
Sodium	110mg
Total Carbohydrate	65g
Dietary Fibre	7g
Sugars	29g
Protein	13g

CHICKPEA & ROOT VEGETABLE HASH

This breakfast hash elevates simple root vegetables and makes them the star. The egg yolk creates a rich sauce for the roasted vegetables.

SERVES 6 · PREP 20 MINS · COOK 30 MINS

2 tbsp coconut oil

1 small sweet potato, peeled and diced

1 turnip, peeled and diced

1 large parsnip, peeled and diced

3 carrots, diced

1 tbsp thyme

pinch of crushed dried chillies

½ tsp ancho chilli powder

350g (12oz) cooked chickpeas

salt and freshly ground black pepper

6 large eggs

1 Preheat the oven to 190°C (375°F). In a large cast-iron, ovenproof frying pan, heat the oil over a medium heat. Once shimmering, add the sweet potato, turnip, parsnip, and carrots. Stir to coat.

2 Add the thyme, crushed dried chillies, and ancho chilli powder. Stir once more, then place the frying pan in the oven and cook for 20 minutes, until the vegetables are tender. Remove from the oven, add the chickpeas, stir, and return to the oven. Cook for 5 more minutes, until the chickpeas are warmed through.

3 Meanwhile, heat a large non-stick frying pan over a medium heat. Crack 1 egg into the frying pan and cook for 3 minutes, or until the white is set but the yolk is runny. Remove and repeat for the remaining 5 eggs.

4 Season the hash with salt and pepper to taste. Divide among 6 serving plates and top each with an egg. Serve immediately.

● Make it with meat

Sauté 75g (2½oz) diced pancetta in coconut oil before adding the root vegetables.

Pulse exchange

If you don't want to use chickpeas, substitute an equal amount of **adzuki beans** or **haricot beans**.

Nutrition per serving

Calories	260
Total Fat	11g
Saturated Fat	6g
Cholesterol	185mg
Sodium	320mg
Total Carbohydrate	28g
Dietary Fibre	7g
Sugars	7g
Protein	12g

YELLOW LENTIL BERRY SMOOTHIE

Having cooked lentils on hand is an easy and undetectable way to quickly add protein – and a boost of rich colour – to your three berry smoothie.

MAKES 2 · PREP 10 MINS

300g (10oz) sliced
  strawberries
75g (2½oz) blueberries
60g (2oz) blackberries
85g (3oz) cooked yellow
  lentils
2 tbsp agave nectar
240ml (8fl oz) milk

1 In a blender, combine the strawberries, blueberries, blackberries, lentils, agave, and milk.

2 Blend until fully combined, then pour into two glasses and serve immediately.

● **Make it vegan**

Instead of milk, substitute vanilla almond milk or coconut milk.

Pulse exchange

For the yellow lentils, substitute an equal amount of **green lentils** or **brown lentils**.

Nutrition per smoothie

Calories	229
Total Fat	3g
Saturated Fat	0g
Cholesterol	0mg
Sodium	49mg
Total Carbohydrate	46g
Dietary Fibre	8g
Sugars	31g
Protein	8g

BLACK BEAN BREAKFAST TOSTADAS

These crunchy fried tortillas are topped with creamy scrambled eggs and spicy, savoury black beans for an irresistible Mexican-style breakfast.

MAKES 4 · PREP 15 MINS · COOK 20 MINS

1 tbsp olive oil

1 small onion, finely diced

1 jalapeño, deseeded and finely diced

1 garlic clove, finely chopped

350g (12oz) cooked black beans

1 tbsp ground cumin

1 tsp chipotle chilli powder

120ml (4fl oz) vegetable stock

salt and freshly ground black pepper

4 corn tostada shells

4 large eggs

½ tbsp double cream

115g (4oz) feta cheese

springs of coriander, to garnish

hot sauce, to garnish

1 Preheat the oven to 170°C (325°F). In a medium frying pan, heat the oil over a medium-low heat. Add the onion and cook for 5 minutes, or until translucent. Add the jalapeño and garlic and cook for an additional 2–3 minutes.

2 Add the black beans, cumin, and chipotle chilli powder and stir to coat. Add the stock, bring to the boil, then reduce to a simmer and cook for 5 minutes, or until the liquid reduces. Season with salt and pepper to taste.

3 Meanwhile, arrange the tostada shells on a baking tray in an even layer, with their edges slightly overlapping. Bake for 2–3 minutes until warmed through.

4 In a small mixing bowl, whisk together the eggs and double cream. In a non-stick frying pan, over a medium-low heat, scramble the eggs to the desired consistency.

5 To assemble, spread equal amounts of the black bean mixture on the tostada shells. Top with equal amounts of scrambled eggs. Sprinkle a quarter of the feta on each tostada, then garnish with coriander and hot sauce. Serve immediately.

● Make it vegan

Instead of eggs, scramble 225g (8oz) firm tofu with salt and pepper.

● Make it with meat

Crumble 1 rasher of crispy bacon over the beans as you assemble the tostadas.

Nutrition per tostada

Calories	430
Total Fat	22g
Saturated Fat	8g
Cholesterol	220mg
Sodium	500mg
Total Carbohydrate	37g
Dietary Fibre	9g
Sugars	3g
Protein	21g

Why not try...
For a boost of healthy fats, top each tostada with wedges of sliced avocado.

SPICY MUNG BEAN SCRAMBLE

Mung beans have a mild taste and creamy texture – they're the perfect addition to this spicy pepper and jalapeño scramble.

● **Make it with meat**

Use any combination of chopped, cooked meat – bacon, chicken, turkey, or ham. Add up to 30g (1oz) per serving, along with the mung beans.

SERVES 4 · PREP 15 MINS · COOK 15 MINS

1 tbsp olive oil

1 orange or yellow pepper, diced

2 spring onions, chopped

1 small jalapeño, deseeded and finely chopped

85g (3oz) cooked mung beans

6 large eggs

salt and freshly ground black pepper

pinch of smoked paprika

1 ripe avocado, thinly sliced

15g (½oz) chopped coriander leaves

15g (½oz) beansprouts (optional)

hot sauce, to serve

1 In a medium non-stick frying pan heat the oil over a medium-low heat. Add the peppers, spring onion, and jalapeño and cook for 3–4 minutes until soft. Stir in the mung beans and cook for an additional 1–2 minutes until warmed through.

2 Meanwhile, in a medium mixing bowl whisk together the eggs, salt and pepper, and paprika. Pour the egg mixture into the frying pan with the cooked vegetables. Using a silicone spatula or wooden spoon, stir the eggs until soft curds begin to form. Continue to cook, stirring frequently, for 4–5 minutes over a medium-low heat until the eggs reach the desired consistency. Remove from the heat.

3 To serve, divide the scrambled eggs among four plates. Garnish each with a quarter of the sliced avocado and chopped coriander. If using, sprinkle the beansprouts on top. Serve immediately, with hot sauce on the side.

Nutrition per serving

Calories	260
Total Fat	19g
Saturated Fat	4g
Cholesterol	280mg
Sodium	280mg
Total Carbohydrate	12g
Dietary Fibre	6g
Sugars	4g
Protein	13g

Why not try...

For a creamier texture, sprinkle in 30g (1oz) grated mature cheddar cheese, midway through cooking the eggs.

ENGLISH BREAKFAST EGG-IN-THE-HOLE

This mash-up of a traditional English breakfast and egg-in-the-hole is an unexpected way to unite two breakfast classics.

● **Make it with meat**

For a meatier English breakfast, add a bacon rasher or a sausage to each plate.

SERVES 4 · PREP 20 MINS · COOK 35 MINS

1 tbsp olive oil

1 small onion, finely diced

1 garlic clove, finely chopped

450g (1lb) cooked haricot beans

300g (10oz) passata

2 tbsp molasses

pinch of crushed dried chillies

salt and freshly ground black pepper

2 plum tomatoes, halved lengthways

225g (8oz) mushrooms, quartered

4 slices of wholewheat bread

4 large eggs

1 To make the baked beans, in a medium saucepan heat the oil over a medium-low heat. Add the onion and cook for 2 minutes. Add the garlic and cook for an additional minute.

2 Stir in the haricot beans, passata, molasses, and crushed dried chillies. Bring to the boil then reduce to a simmer and cook for 20 minutes. Season with salt and pepper to taste.

3 Meanwhile, heat a large non-stick frying pan over a medium heat. Sear the tomatoes, cut-side down, for 3–4 minutes, until lightly cooked. Remove and set aside on serving plates. Add the mushrooms to the frying pan. Season and cook for 3–4 minutes, until tender. Remove and place on the serving plates. Wipe out the frying pan and return to a medium-low heat.

4 With a 5cm (2in) round cookie cutter, cut a hole out of the middle of each slice of bread. Place two slices of bread, along with their cut-out circles, in the frying pan. Toast for 2 minutes, then turn over. Crack 1 egg into each hole and cook for 3–5 minutes until the whites are set and the yolks are cooked as desired. Remove from the frying pan and repeat with the remaining 2 slices of bread and eggs.

5 Place each egg-in-the-hole on a serving plate and top with baked beans. Serve each with a roasted tomato half and a quarter of the sautéed mushrooms.

Nutrition per serving

Calories	380
Total Fat	10g
Saturated Fat	2.5g
Cholesterol	185mg
Sodium	230mg
Total Carbohydrate	54g
Dietary Fibre	14g
Sugars	15g
Protein	20g

ASPARAGUS & GREEN LENTILS
WITH POACHED EGG

This impressive-looking brunch dish couldn't be easier to prepare. The yolk from the poached egg makes a luxurious sauce for the roasted asparagus and lentils.

SERVES 4 · PREP 10 MINS · COOK 15 MINS

450g (1lb) fine asparagus, woody ends trimmed

2 tbsp olive oil

salt and freshly ground black pepper

2½ tbsp red wine vinegar

1 tbsp Dijon mustard

¼ tsp chopped thyme

⅛ tsp of white vinegar

400g (14oz) cooked green lentils

4 large eggs

1 Preheat the oven to 180°C (350°F). Toss the asparagus with 1 tablespoon of oil. Arrange on a baking tray in a single layer and season with salt and pepper. Roast for 10 minutes, or until tender.

2 Meanwhile, to make the dressing, in a medium bowl combine the red wine vinegar, Dijon mustard, thyme, and remaining 1 tablespoon of oil. Whisk until emulsified. Add the lentils and stir to combine. Set aside and let the lentils absorb the dressing.

3 To poach the eggs, fill a large saucepan with water, about 4cm (1½in) deep. Bring to the boil then reduce to a simmer. Add the white vinegar. One at a time, crack each egg into a ramekin and gently tip it into the water. Cook for 3 minutes. Drain and place on a plate lined with kitchen paper.

4 To serve, divide the asparagus among 4 plates and top each with the lentils. Place 1 poached egg atop the lentils. Season with pepper and serve immediately.

Nutrition per serving

Calories	238
Total Fat	12.5g
Saturated Fat	2.6g
Cholesterol	183mg
Sodium	195mg
Total Carbohydrate	19g
Dietary Fibre	6g
Sugars	3.7g
Protein	15g

Pulse exchange

Substitute an equal amount of **brown lentils** or **mung beans** for the green lentils.

RED LENTIL SHAKSHUKA

This comforting, one-pan meal is a traditional Middle Eastern breakfast of eggs baked in spicy tomato sauce. The red lentils add a hearty texture and nutty taste.

SERVES 4 · PREP 25 MINS · COOK 30 MINS

2 tbsp olive oil

1 small onion, diced

1 red pepper, deseeded and chopped

2 garlic cloves, finely chopped

1 red Thai chilli, deseeded and finely chopped

2 x 400g (14oz) cans chopped tomatoes

1 tbsp tomato purée

1 tsp ground cumin

¾ tsp smoked paprika

2 tbsp red wine vinegar

45g (1½oz) uncooked red lentils

salt and freshly ground black pepper

4 large eggs

3 tbsp chopped flat-leaf parsley

1 In a 25cm (10in) cast-iron frying pan, warm the oil over a medium-low heat until shimmering. Add the onion and pepper and cook for 5 minutes, or until soft. Add the garlic and chilli and continue to cook for 1–2 minutes, until fragrant.

2 Add the tomatoes, tomato purée, cumin, paprika, and vinegar and stir to combine. Cook for 5 minutes, or until warmed through. Add the lentils and cook, covered, for 20–25 minutes, until tender. Season with salt and pepper to taste.

3 With the back of a spoon, press to create 4 wells in the tomato-lentil mixture in the frying pan. Crack 1 egg into each well. Cover the frying pan and cook for 5–8 minutes until the eggs are just set. Sprinkle with parsley and serve immediately.

Nutrition per serving

Calories	240
Total Fat	12g
Saturated Fat	2.5g
Cholesterol	185mg
Sodium	280mg
Total Carbohydrate	21g
Dietary Fibre	5g
Sugars	8g
Protein	11g

● **Make it vegan**

Omit the eggs and use tofu rounds, firmly pressed and cut into four 1cm (½in) slices.

MASCARPONE-STUFFED FRENCH TOAST

The creamy, tangy filling of this decadent French toast is perfectly complemented by the bright citrus notes of the blood orange sauce.

MAKES 4 · PREP 30 MINS · COOK 30 MINS

- 350g (12oz) cooked cannellini beans
- 2 tbsp sugar
- 6oz (170g) mascarpone, softened
- ½ tbsp plus 1 tsp vanilla extract
- zest of 2 large blood oranges
- 120ml (4fl oz) agave nectar
- 120ml (4fl oz) blood orange juice (juice of 4 small blood oranges)
- 1 tsp cornflour
- 1 tbsp unsalted butter
- 1 large egg
- 180ml (6fl oz) unsweetened almond milk
- ¼ tsp cinnamon
- pinch of salt
- 1 loaf of challah bread, about 400–450g (14–16oz)
- icing sugar, to garnish

1 To make the filling, in a food processor combine the cannellini beans, sugar, mascarpone, ½ tablespoon of vanilla extract, and blood orange zest. Pulse until thoroughly combined. Transfer to a small bowl and refrigerate for at least 1 hour or overnight.

2 To make the blood orange sauce, in a small saucepan whisk together the agave, orange juice, and cornflour until smooth. Boil gently for 3–4 minutes until slightly thickened. Remove from the heat and stir in the butter.

3 To make the batter, in a large mixing bowl whisk together the egg, almond milk, cinnamon, and salt. Set aside.

4 Trim the narrow ends from the challah to create an evenly sized loaf. Cut the loaf into four 5cm (2in) slices. To create pockets for the filling, with a small knife cut a slit in the centre of each slice without cutting through completely. Stuff each slice with 2 heaped tablespoons of filling and press the cut to seal. Soak each slice in batter for 1 minute on each side.

5 Heat a non-stick frying pan over a medium heat. In batches, cook the slices for 2–3 minutes on each side, until golden brown. Garnish with icing sugar, top with the blood orange sauce, and serve immediately.

Nutrition per French toast

Calories	650
Total Fat	19g
Saturated Fat	140g
Cholesterol	95mg
Sodium	670mg
Total Carbohydrate	98g
Dietary Fibre	9g
Sugars	29g
Protein	22g

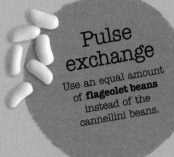

Pulse exchange

Use an equal amount of **flageolet beans** instead of the cannellini beans.

YELLOW LENTIL EGG MUFFINS

These cheesy egg muffins with sweet broccoli florets are an easy grab-and-go breakfast.

MAKES 12 · PREP 15 MINS · COOK 30 MINS

175g (6oz) broccoli florets, finely chopped
10 large eggs
115g (4oz) cooked yellow lentils
75g (2½oz) mature Cheddar cheese, grated

60g (2oz) roasted red peppers, diced
pinch of paprika
salt and freshly ground black pepper

1 Preheat the oven to 180°C (350°F). Heat a frying pan over a medium-low heat. Add the broccoli and cook for 2–3 minutes, until bright green but still crisp. Remove from the heat and let cool slightly.

2 In a large mixing bowl, whisk the eggs. Add the broccoli, lentils, Cheddar, red peppers, and paprika. Season with salt and pepper.

3 Grease thoroughly each cup of a 12-cup muffin pan. Divide the egg mixture evenly among the cups.

4 Bake for 20 minutes, or until completely set. Run a blunt knife around each muffin to release. Serve immediately or let cool and store in an airtight container in the fridge for up to 2 days.

Nutrition per muffin

Calories	100
Total Fat	6g
Saturated Fat	2.5g
Cholesterol	160mg
Sodium	310mg
Total Carbohydrate	3g
Dietary Fibre	1g
Sugars	<1g
Protein	8g

● **Make it with meat**

Add 75g (2½oz) cooked and diced ham or bacon to the egg mixture before baking.

BLACK BEAN COCOA SMOOTHIE

Black beans and chocolate are an unusual match in this smoothie, which is both a sweet treat and a healthy start to your day.

MAKES 2 · PREP 10 MINS

240ml (8fl oz) milk
85g (3oz) cooked black beans
1 large, ripe banana

3 tbsp unsweetened cocoa powder
1 tbsp agave nectar
75g (2½oz) crushed ice cubes

1 In a blender, add the milk and black beans. Blend until smooth.

2 Add the banana, cocoa powder, agave, and crushed ice. Blend again until smooth. Pour into 2 glasses and serve immediately.

Nutrition per smoothie

Calories	240
Total Fat	4g
Saturated Fat	1g
Cholesterol	0mg
Sodium	55mg
Total Carbohydrate	45g
Dietary Fibre	8g
Sugars	21g
Protein	12g

● **Make it vegan**

Replace the milk with an equal amount of unsweetened soya or almond milk.

SPICED APPLE & MUNG BEAN MUFFINS

Mung beans puréed with apple sauce make for one of the moistest muffins you'll ever taste and provide protein and fibre for a filling on-the-go breakfast.

MAKES 12 · PREP 35 MINS · COOK 20 MINS

150g (5½oz) unsweetened apple sauce

85g (3oz) cooked mung beans

2 tbsp agave nectar

100g (3½oz) wholemeal flour

100g (3½oz) plain flour

2 tsp baking powder

1 tsp cinnamon

pinch of ground nutmeg

1 large egg

100g (3½oz) light brown sugar

80ml (3fl oz) unsweetened almond milk

1 medium Granny Smith apple, peeled, cored, and finely diced

20g (¾oz) rolled oats

1 Preheat the oven to 175°C (350°F). In a food processor, combine the apple sauce, mung beans, and agave. Purée until smooth.

2 In a large mixing bowl, whisk together the wholemeal flour, plain flour, baking powder, cinnamon, and nutmeg.

3 In a medium mixing bowl, add the egg, brown sugar, almond milk, and apple sauce-mung bean mixture. Whisk until thoroughly combined.

4 Add the bean mixture to the flour mixture and stir until no streaks of dry ingredients remain. Gently fold in the diced apples until combined.

5 Line a 12-cup muffin pan with paper liners. Place 2 tablespoons of the mixture into each cup. Sprinkle the top of each muffin with 1 teaspoon of oats. Bake for 20–25 minutes until set, and a skewer inserted into the centre of the muffin comes out clean. Let rest for an hour before serving. Store in an airtight container for up to 2 days.

Nutrition per muffin

Calories	110
Total Fat	0.5g
Saturated Fat	0g
Cholesterol	0mg
Sodium	5mg
Total Carbohydrate	25g
Dietary Fibre	2g
Sugars	10g
Protein	2g

● **Make it vegan**

Substitute half a mashed banana for the egg.

YELLOW LENTIL WAFFLES
WITH FIVE SPICE BERRY SAUCE

Crispy on the outside, soft and light on the inside, these wholesome waffles have a slightly nutty flavour. The five spice powder in the sauce brings out the sweetness of the berries.

MAKES 4 · PREP 15 MINS · COOK 15 MINS

175g (6oz) fresh raspberries

175g (6oz) fresh blackberries

175g (6oz) fresh blueberries

¼ tsp five spice powder

1 cinnamon stick

3 tbsp water

300ml (10fl oz) unsweetened almond milk

60ml (2fl oz) rapeseed oil

2 tsp vanilla extract

3 tbsp agave nectar

225g (8oz) wholemeal flour

1½ tsp baking powder

115g (4oz) cooked yellow lentils

1 In a small saucepan, combine the raspberries, blackberries, blueberries, five spice powder, and cinnamon stick. Cover and cook over a low heat for 15 minutes, stirring regularly, until the berries break down into a thickened sauce. Add 2–3 tablespoons of water as needed.

2 Meanwhile, in a small bowl whisk together the almond milk, oil, vanilla, and agave.

3 Preheat a waffle maker. In a large mixing bowl, combine the flour and baking powder. Incorporate the almond milk mixture into the flour mixture. Gently fold in the lentils.

4 When the waffle iron is hot, spray it with cooking spray. Add 120ml (4fl oz) batter to each section and cook, according to the manufacturer's instructions, to make 4 waffles in total.

5 Remove the cinnamon stick from the sauce. Serve the waffles and sauce immediately.

Nutrition per waffle

Calories	350
Total Fat	10g
Saturated Fat	0.5g
Cholesterol	0mg
Sodium	80mg
Total Carbohydrate	50g
Dietary Fibre	13g
Sugars	6g
Protein	13g

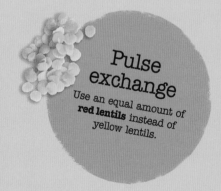

Pulse exchange
Use an equal amount of **red lentils** instead of yellow lentils.

MOTH BEAN GREEN SMOOTHIE

Adding moth beans to your green smoothie is a simple way to fortify your morning drink with additional protein and fibre.

MAKES 2 · PREP 10 MINS

160ml (5fl oz) unsweetened almond milk or soya milk

200g (7oz) diced fresh pineapple

45g (1½oz) baby spinach

100g (3½oz) cooked moth beans, or black lentils

1 ripe banana

45g (1½oz) crushed ice cubes

1 Using a blender, pour in the almond milk, then add the pineapple, spinach, moth beans, and banana. Blend until smooth.

2 Add the crushed ice and blend again until smooth. Pour the smoothie into 2 glasses and serve immediately.

Nutrition per smoothie

Calories	160	Sodium	85mg
Total Fat	1.5g	Total Carbohydrate	37g
Saturated Fat	0g	Dietary Fibre	6g
Cholesterol	0mg	Sugars	19g
		Protein	5g

LEMON POPPY SEED PANCAKES

Poppy seeds add unexpected texture to these deliciously fluffy pancakes.

MAKES 4 · PREP 30 MINS · COOK 20 MINS

80ml (3fl oz) unsweetened almond milk

3 tbsp lemon juice

zest of 2 lemons

2 tbsp fluid coconut oil

1 tsp vanilla extract

2½ tbsp sugar

1 tsp bicarbonate of soda

1 tsp baking powder

100g (3½oz) chickpea flour

1 tbsp poppy seeds

1 In a small mixing bowl, combine the almond milk, lemon juice, lemon zest, coconut oil, vanilla extract, and sugar.

2 In a large mixing bowl, whisk together the bicarbonate of soda, baking powder, chickpea flour, and poppy seeds. Pour the almond milk mixture into the flour mixture and stir gently until smooth. Gently fold in the poppy seeds until combined. Let the batter rest for 10 minutes without stirring.

3 Heat a medium non-stick frying pan over a medium heat. Pour a quarter of the batter into the frying pan. Cook for 2 minutes, or until bubbles form along the edge and in the centre of the pancake. Gently flip and cook for an additional 1–2 minutes. Remove from the heat and repeat with the remaining batter to make 4 pancakes in total. Serve immediately with butter or maple syrup.

Nutrition per pancake

Calories	140	Sodium	240mg
Total Fat	7g	Total Carbohydrate	16g
Saturated Fat	4g	Dietary Fibre	2g
Cholesterol	0mg	Sugars	6g
		Protein	4g

BEAN & QUINOA BREAKFAST BOWLS

Kidney beans simmered with herbs and spices create a flavourful base for these hearty, satisfying breakfast bowls.

SERVES 8 · PREP 15 MINS · COOK 1 HR 30 MINS

1 tbsp vegetable oil

1 onion, chopped

1 green pepper, deseeded and chopped

2 celery sticks, diced

2 garlic cloves, finely chopped

2 bay leaves

4 sprigs of thyme

450g (1lb) soaked kidney beans

2 litres (3½ pints) vegetable stock

¾ tsp ground cayenne pepper

¾ tsp smoked paprika

salt and freshly ground black pepper

175g (6oz) uncooked quinoa

1 large avocado, sliced

30g (1oz) coriander leaves

hot sauce (optional)

1 In a large flameproof casserole or stock pot, heat the oil over a medium-low heat until shimmering. Add the onion, green pepper, and celery. Cook for 2–3 minutes until soft. Add the garlic and cook for an additional 1–2 minutes.

2 Add the bay leaves, thyme, and soaked kidney beans. Stir in 1.5 litres (2½ pints) of the stock, the cayenne and paprika. Bring to the boil then reduce the heat and simmer, covered, for 1–1¼ hours, stirring occasionally, until the beans are tender. Season with salt and pepper to taste.

3 Meanwhile, in a separate pan, bring the remaining 500ml (1 pint) of stock to the boil over a medium heat. Stir in the quinoa and return to the boil. Reduce the heat to low and cook, covered, for 20 minutes, or until all the stock is absorbed. Remove from the heat and let sit, covered.

4 Remove the bay leaf and thyme stems from the bean mixture. To serve, use a slotted spoon to divide the quinoa into bowls. Top with the bean mixture, adding cooking liquid as desired. Garnish with avocado and coriander. Serve immediately, with hot sauce, if using.

● Make it with meat

Add 60g (2oz) chopped smoked bacon and cook along with the onions in step 1.

Nutrition per serving

Calories	400
Total Fat	8g
Saturated Fat	2g
Cholesterol	0mg
Sodium	160mg
Total Carbohydrate	65g
Dietary Fibre	16g
Sugars	6g
Protein	20g

Why not try...
For added richness, top each bowl with a fried egg – the yolk makes an excellent sauce for the beans and quinoa.

TROPICAL SMOOTHIE BOWL

The bright flavours of pineapple and mango are complemented by velvety white beans and banana in these beautiful, protein-rich bowls.

● **Make it vegan**

Use a vegan yogurt alternative rather than vanilla yogurt.

MAKES 2 · PREP 10 MINS

175g (6oz) diced mango

200g (7oz) diced pineapple

1 banana, sliced

1 tbsp honey or agave nectar

200g (7oz) low-fat vanilla yogurt

85g (3oz) cooked cannellini beans

15g (½oz) toasted coconut, to garnish

2 tsp chia seeds, to garnish

1 Withhold a bit of mango, pineapple, and banana for the garnish. In a blender, add the remainder of the fruit, along with the honey, yogurt, and cannellini beans. Purée until completely smooth.

2 Divide the smoothie between 2 bowls, and garnish with toasted coconut, chia seeds, and the reserved mango, pineapple, and banana. Serve immediately.

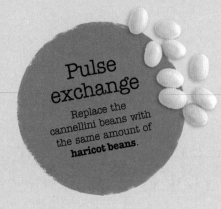

Pulse exchange

Replace the cannellini beans with the same amount of **haricot beans**.

Nutrition per bowl

Calories	370
Total Fat	7g
Saturated Fat	4.5g
Cholesterol	<5mg
Sodium	95mg
Total Carbohydrate	72g
Dietary Fibre	9g
Sugars	51g
Protein	9g

SNACKS
& SPREADS

MUNG BEAN GUACAMOLE

The addition of mung beans brings a nutritional boost and an extra creamy texture to this Mexican classic. Serve with tortilla chips or alongside some tacos.

SERVES 2 · PREP 20 MINS

2 large avocados

juice of 1 lime

1 onion, finely chopped

2 garlic cloves, finely chopped

1 tomato, diced

85g (3oz) cooked mung beans

2 tbsp roughly chopped coriander leaves

salt and freshly ground black pepper

1 Cut the avocados in half, remove the stones, and scoop the flesh into a large bowl. Immediately add the lime juice. With a pastry cutter or fork, roughly mash the avocado.

2 Add the onion, garlic, tomato, mung beans, and coriander. Stir gently to combine. Season with salt and pepper to taste. Serve immediately.

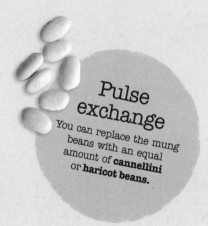

Pulse exchange

You can replace the mung beans with an equal amount of **cannellini** or **haricot beans.**

Nutrition per serving

Calories	300
Total Fat	21g
Saturated Fat	3g
Cholesterol	0mg
Sodium	170mg
Total Carbohydrate	25g
Dietary Fibre	15g
Sugars	4g
Protein	7g

YELLOW LENTIL DEVILLED EGGS

Basil, oregano, and lemon juice brighten these devilled eggs, a picnic and party favourite. Incorporating yellow lentils updates the recipe and adds texture to the filling.

MAKES 12 · PREP 20 MINS · COOK 10 MINS

6 large eggs

85g (3oz) cooked yellow lentils

60ml (2fl oz) mayonnaise or sour cream

¾ tsp Dijon mustard

5g (⅛oz) chopped basil leaves

10g (¼oz) chopped oregano

½ tbsp lemon juice

salt and freshly ground black pepper

chopped chervil or chopped chives, to garnish

1 Bring a large saucepan of water to a rapid boil and carefully lower the eggs into the water. Boil for 9 minutes, then quickly remove and place in an ice bath to cool completely.

2 Peel off the shells and slice the eggs in half lengthways. Scoop out the yolks. Reserve the whites to fill.

3 To make the filling, in a food processor add the yolks, lentils, mayonnaise, mustard, basil, and oregano. Process on low, slowly drizzling in the lemon juice. Purée until smooth. Season with salt and pepper to taste.

4 Carefully spoon or pipe about 1 tablespoon of filling into each egg half. Garnish with chervil or chives. Serve immediately, or keep in an airtight container in the fridge for up to 2 days.

Nutrition per egg

Calories	80
Total Fat	6g
Saturated Fat	1.5g
Cholesterol	95mg
Sodium	160mg
Total Carbohydrate	3g
Dietary Fibre	1g
Sugars	0g
Protein	4g

● **Make it with meat**

Garnish the devilled eggs with 2 tablespoons of colourful orange tobiko or salmon roe.

ADZUKI BEAN SUMMER ROLLS
WITH PEANUT SAUCE

Spiralized jicama replaces traditional rice noodles in these summer rolls. Adzuki beans complement the sweet mango and creamy avocado.

MAKES 16 · PREP 1 HR

125g (4½oz) smooth peanut butter

juice of 1 lime

1 tbsp rice wine vinegar

80ml (3fl oz) water

½ tsp Sriracha

1 small jicama, peeled (if you can't find jicama, try using water chestnuts or Jerusalem artichoke)

25g (1oz) mint leaves

1 mango, peeled, stoned, and cut into 1cm (½in) slices

1 small red onion, julienned

1 avocado, pitted and cut into 5mm (¼in) slices

325g (11oz) cooked adzuki beans

60g (2oz) coriander leaves

1 packet of spring roll rice paper wrappers

●Make it with meat

Horizontally slice 1 cooked king prawn for each roll, and place atop the mint during assembly.

1 To make the peanut sauce, in a small bowl whisk together the peanut butter, lime juice, vinegar, water, and Sriracha until smooth. Set aside until ready to serve.

2 Cut the jicama into even chunks. Adjust a spiralizer to the thinnest blade and spiralize the jicama. Set out the jicama, mint, mango, onion, avocado, adzuki beans, and coriander on your worktop to prepare for filling the rolls.

3 Pour warm water into a shallow flan or pie dish. One at a time, submerge the rice paper wrapper into warm water for 30 seconds, or until pliable without tearing. Remove from the water and place onto a clean, flat, non-stick surface, such as a plastic or ceramic cutting board.

4 Arrange the desired amount of mint leaves, mango, red onion, avocado, adzuki beans, coriander, and spiralized jicama in the centre of the wrapper, working quickly so that it doesn't dry out. Do not overstuff the wrapper, or it will tear. Fold the bottom edge over the filling, and press to seal. Then fold the sides towards the centre, tucking in the filling. Roll gently and seal firmly.

5 Repeat to use all the remaining ingredients. Serve with peanut sauce on the side. Store in the fridge for 2–3 days, individually wrapped so they do not stick together.

Nutrition per summer roll

Calories	178
Total Fat	6g
Saturated Fat	1g
Cholesterol	0mg
Sodium	40mg
Total Carbohydrate	25g
Dietary Fibre	4g
Sugars	1g
Protein	4g

LEMONY SPINACH HUMMUS

The bold green colour of this citrusy hummus screams healthy. Its bright, fresh flavour tastes great with pitta bread, or as a spread for wraps and sandwiches.

SERVES 6 · PREP 5 MINS · COOK 5 MINS

150g (5½oz) cooked chickpeas, peeled

75g (2½oz) baby spinach

2 garlic cloves

juice and zest of 1 large lemon

1 tbsp tahini

60ml (2fl oz) olive oil

salt and freshly ground black pepper

1½ tbsp chia seeds, to garnish

alfalfa sprouts, to garnish

microgreens, to garnish

1 In a food processor combine the chickpeas, spinach, garlic, lemon juice and zest, and tahini. Process on low for 1 minute to combine the ingredients.

2 With the processor on high, drizzle in the oil.For a thinner consistency, gradually add cold water, 1 tablespoon at a time, until the desired texture is achieved.

3 Transfer to a serving bowl and garnish with chia seeds, sprouts, and microgreens. Serve immediately.

●Make it with meat

For a meaty appetizer, top with 225g (8oz) sautéed minced lamb, spiced as desired.

Nutrition per serving

Calories	140
Total Fat	10g
Saturated Fat	1.5g
Cholesterol	0mg
Sodium	20mg
Total Carbohydrate	11g
Dietary Fibre	4g
Sugars	2g
Protein	4g

Pulse exchange

Substitute an equal amount of **cannellini** or **haricot beans** for the chickpeas.

BELUGA LENTIL & OLIVE TAPENADE

This olive spread from the south of France is a flavour-packed appetizer. Serve it with a toasted baguette or crudités.

SERVES 6 · PREP 5 MINS · COOK 5 MINS

140g (5oz) kalamata
  olives, pitted
150g (5½oz) cooked
  beluga lentils

2 garlic cloves
1½ tbsp capers, drained
60ml (2fl oz) olive oil

1 In a food processor, add the olives, lentils, garlic, and capers. Pulse to combine.

2 With the processor running on low, drizzle in the oil until smooth and fully combined. Serve immediately, or store in an airtight container in the fridge for up to 3 days.

Nutrition per serving

Calories	220
Total Fat	12g
Saturated Fat	1.5g
Cholesterol	0mg
Sodium	105mg
Total Carbohydrate	23g
Dietary Fibre	6g
Sugars	<1g
Protein	8g

● **Make it with meat**

Add 2 canned anchovy fillets to the mixture for an extra briny punch.

BLACK-EYED BEAN HUMMUS

This dip has a light, whipped texture that tastes great with crunchy cucumber slices and radishes, or toasted pitta bread.

SERVES 6 · PREP 15 MINS

400g (14oz) cooked
  black-eyed beans
3 tbsp tahini
1 garlic clove
juice of 1 lemon

¼ tsp smoked paprika
60ml (2fl oz) olive oil
salt and freshly ground
  black pepper

1 Set aside 2 tablespoons of black-eyed beans for the garnish. In a food processor combine the remaining black-eyed beans, tahini, garlic, lemon juice, and paprika. Pulse to incorporate.

2 With the processor running on low, drizzle in the oil until smooth. For a thinner consistency, add up to 60ml (2fl oz) water and blend until smooth. Season with salt and pepper to taste and pulse once more to incorporate.

3 Transfer to a serving bowl and garnish with the reserved 2 tablespoons of black-eyed beans and a pinch of smoked paprika. Serve immediately or store in an airtight container in the fridge for up to 2 days.

Nutrition per serving

Calories	170
Total Fat	11g
Saturated Fat	1.5g
Cholesterol	0mg
Sodium	105mg
Total Carbohydrate	14g
Dietary Fibre	3g
Sugars	<1g
Protein	6g

CHICKPEA FRIES

A satisfying, salty snack, the fried chickpea batter in this recipe creates fries with a thin, crispy exterior and a lightly spiced, silky interior.

● **Make it with meat**

For greater depth of flavour, use chicken stock rather than vegetable stock.

SERVES 6 · PREP 5 MINS, PLUS 2 HRS TO CHILL · COOK 10 MINS

115g (4oz) chickpea flour

500ml (16fl oz) vegetable stock

¼ tsp garam masala

pinch of cinnamon

500ml (16fl oz) vegetable oil or rapeseed oil

salt and freshly ground black pepper

1 Lightly grease a 20 x 20cm (8 x 8in) glass baking dish, and set aside.

2 In a saucepan combine the chickpea flour, stock, garam masala, and cinnamon over a medium-low heat. Bring to the boil then reduce to a simmer. Cook, covered, for 8–9 minutes, whisking constantly, until the mixture thickens to the consistency of smooth peanut butter.

3 Remove from the heat. Transfer to the prepared baking dish and spread evenly. Cover with foil or cling film and refrigerate for 2 hours or overnight, until completely set.

4 Turn the dish upside down to release the mixture onto a clean, flat work surface. Blot both sides with kitchen paper to remove excess moisture. Cut the square in half, then cut each half into 12–14 narrow rectangles, to make 24–28 fries.

5 Line a baking sheet with kitchen paper. In a heavy-based 23cm (9in) frying pan, heat the oil over a medium heat until hot and shimmering. Add the chickpea fries in batches so they form an even layer. Cook for 2–3 minutes on each side until golden brown. Transfer to the baking sheet to absorb excess oil. Repeat to cook the remaining fries. Season with salt and pepper and serve immediately.

Nutrition per serving

Calories	220
Total Fat	19g
Saturated Fat	15g
Cholesterol	0mg
Sodium	55mg
Total Carbohydrate	10g
Dietary Fibre	2g
Sugars	2g
Protein	3g

Why not try...
For an unusual treat, dust these fries with icing sugar to give them a sweet and salty flavour contrast.

SPICY CARROT HUMMUS

Harissa is a natural match for the sweetness of carrots and the tang of tahini in this hummus. Serve with crisp vegetables or seeded crackers.

SERVES 6 · PREP 20 MINS · COOK 30 MINS

350g (12oz) carrots, ends trimmed, around 7–8 carrots

60ml (2fl oz) olive oil, plus 1 tbsp for roasting

350g (12oz) cooked chickpeas, peeled

1 tbsp water

1½ tbsp tahini

juice of 1 large lime

1 tbsp harissa paste

salt and freshly ground black pepper

1 Preheat the oven to 180°C (350°F). Peel the carrots and cut into 3cm (1in) chunks. Toss with 1 tablespoon of oil and arrange in a single layer on a baking tray. Roast for 25–30 minutes, until caramelized and tender. Remove from the oven and leave to cool.

2 In a food processor, combine the chickpeas and water and whizz briefly to combine. Add the tahini, lime juice, harissa, and roasted carrots. With the processor running on low, drizzle in the oil. Season with salt and pepper to taste, then pulse a few more times to combine. Serve immediately.

Pulse exchange

Replace the chickpeas with an equal amount of cooked **cannellini** or **haricot beans.**

Nutrition per serving

Calories	240
Total Fat	16g
Saturated Fat	2g
Cholesterol	0mg
Sodium	250mg
Total Carbohydrate	22g
Dietary Fibre	6g
Sugars	6g
Protein	6g

WHITE BEAN BUTTER
WITH RADISHES

Radishes with butter and salt are a classic French snack. Here, the butter is browned and blended with white beans to make a luxurious and creamy dip.

SERVES 4 · PREP 5 MINS · COOK 10 MINS

2 tbsp unsalted butter

175g (6oz) cooked cannellini beans

1 garlic clove

1 tsp water (optional)

1 bunch radishes, washed and tops removed

flaky sea salt

1 In a small saucepan, melt the butter over a low heat. Cook until the butter takes on a light brown colour and nutty aroma, then remove from the heat.

2 In a food processor, combine the butter, cannellini beans, and garlic. Blend on high until smooth, adding water as needed to reach the desired consistency.

3 Transfer the dip to a small bowl and serve alongside radishes and a small dish of sea salt.

Nutrition per serving

Calories	110
Total Fat	6g
Saturated Fat	3.5g
Cholesterol	15mg
Sodium	10mg
Total Carbohydrate	10g
Dietary Fibre	3g
Sugars	<1g
Protein	4g

● **Make it vegan**

Omit the butter for a more traditional white bean dip.

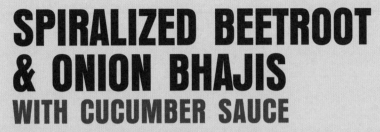

SPIRALIZED BEETROOT & ONION BHAJIS
WITH CUCUMBER SAUCE

These crispy Indian fritters can be eaten as an appetizer or snack. The spiralized beetroot adds a vivid pink colour.

MAKES 12 · PREP 15 MINS · COOK 15 MINS

1 litre (1¾ pints) rapeseed oil

200g (7oz) plain Greek-style yogurt

1 small cucumber, peeled and grated

1 large onion, peeled

1 large beetroot, peeled

pinch of turmeric

½ tsp salt

75g (2½ oz) chickpea flour

120ml (4fl oz) water

1 In a large flameproof casserole or heavy-based saucepan, heat the rapeseed oil over a medium-low heat. Measuring with a deep frying thermometer, bring to 180°C (350°F).

2 Meanwhile, to make the cucumber sauce, in a small bowl stir together the yogurt and cucumber.

3 Adjust a spiralizer to the thinnest blade and spiralize the onion and beetroot. With kitchen scissors, trim into 3cm (1in) lengths.

4 In a large mixing bowl, whisk together the turmeric, salt, chickpea flour, and water. Gradually add water to reach the consistency of pancake batter. Add the beetroot and onion and toss to combine.

5 With your hands, gather 2 tablespoons of the bhaji mixture and carefully drop into the oil. Fry for 4 minutes, or until golden and crispy, rotating once. Place on a plate lined with kitchen paper and repeat with the remaining batter. Serve immediately with the cucumber sauce.

Nutrition per bhaji

Calories	210
Total Fat	19g
Saturated Fat	1.5g
Cholesterol	0mg
Sodium	110mg
Total Carbohydrate	7g
Dietary Fibre	1g
Sugars	3g
Protein	4g

● **Make it vegan**

Replace the Greek-style yogurt in the sauce with the same quantity of coconut milk yogurt.

HARICOT BEAN & ARTICHOKE PAN BAGNAT

This French sandwich is the ultimate picnic or packed lunch recipe. It gets better the longer it sits, as the bread absorbs the vinaigrette and vegetable flavours.

MAKES 4 · PREP 50 MINS

3 tbsp red wine vinegar

1½ tbsp olive oil

1 small cucumber, peeled, deseeded, and thinly sliced

1 small red onion, thinly sliced

390g (14oz) can artichoke hearts

225g (8oz) cooked haricot beans

2 garlic cloves

60g (2oz) cornichons

5g (¼oz) flat-leaf parsley leaves

2 tbsp Greek-style yogurt

pinch of crushed dried chillies

1 wholemeal baguette

12 large basil leaves

1 plum tomato, thinly sliced

2 hard-boiled eggs, thinly sliced

45g (1½oz) pitted Niçoise olives, roughly chopped

Nutrition per sandwich

Calories	320
Total Fat	6g
Saturated Fat	1g
Cholesterol	0mg
Sodium	920mg
Total Carbohydrate	52g
Dietary Fibre	11g
Sugars	6g
Protein	13g

1 In a medium mixing bowl, combine the red wine vinegar, oil, cucumber, and red onion. Toss to combine and set aside to marinate.

2 In a food processor, combine the artichoke hearts, haricot beans, garlic, cornichons, parsley, yogurt, and crushed dried chillies. Pulse until combined but not smooth. Season with salt and pepper to taste.

3 Slice the baguette in half lengthways. Lay the two halves cut-side up on the work surface. To make space for the filling, remove about a 3cm (1in) wide channel of bread from each half.

4 On the bottom half of the baguette, arrange the basil leaves in a single layer. Top with the artichoke bean mixture in an even layer. Then add the slices of plum tomato and hard-boiled egg.

5 On the top half of the baguette, evenly spread the cucumber and red onion mixture. Drizzle on any remaining liquid. Top with Niçoise olives.

6 Carefully place the top half of the baguette on the bottom half. Slice into 4 equal sandwiches. Wrap each in greaseproof paper and leave to marinate in the fridge for at least 30 minutes or overnight.

Make it vegan

Omit the egg and use a dairy-free yogurt rather than Greek yogurt.

Make it with meat

For more briny flavour, add 8 canned anchovy fillets with the olives.

SUMAC ROASTED CHICKPEAS

Salty, tangy, and crispy, these roasted chickpeas are an addictive healthy snack.

SERVES 4 · PREP 5 MINS · COOK 1 HR

2 tbsp olive oil
zest and juice of 2 lemons
2 tsp sumac
1 tsp sea salt

675g (1½lb) cooked chickpeas, thoroughly drained and dried

1 Preheat the oven to 190°C (375°F). In a large mixing bowl, combine the oil, lemon zest and juice, sumac, and salt. Add the chickpeas and toss to coat thoroughly. Spread the chickpeas in an even layer on a baking tray.

2 Bake for 40–45 minutes until golden brown and lightly crisp, stirring every 10–15 minutes. Remove the tray from the oven and place it on a wire rack. Let the chickpeas cool completely on the tray. Serve immediately or store in an airtight container for up to 3 days.

CHICKPEA ENERGY BITES

These peanut butter energy bites are a wonderful make-ahead snack for lunches or mid-afternoon treats.

MAKES 24 · PREP 20 MINS, PLUS 1 HR TO SET

350g (12oz) cooked chickpeas
125g (4½oz) smooth peanut butter
45g (1½oz) rolled oats

80ml (3fl oz) agave nectar
1 tsp vanilla extract
1 tsp cinnamon
pinch of salt

1 In a food processor, pulse the chickpeas until coarsely ground. Transfer to a large mixing bowl. Stir in the peanut butter, oats, agave, vanilla extract, cinnamon, and salt.

2 Take 1 heaped tablespoon of the chickpea mixture and roll into a ball with your hands. Repeat with the remaining chickpea mixture to make 24 in total. Chill to set in an airtight container in the fridge for at least 1 hour, or overnight, before serving.

Nutrition per serving

Calories	330	Sodium	570mg
Total Fat	11g	Total Carbohydrate	47g
Saturated Fat	1.5g	Dietary Fibre	13g
		Sugars	8g
Cholesterol	0mg	Protein	15g

Nutrition per bite

Calories	70	Sodium	45mg
Total Fat	3g	Total Carbohydrate	10g
Saturated Fat	0g	Dietary Fibre	2g
		Sugars	5g
Cholesterol	0mg	Protein	3g

QUINOA & MOTH BEAN DOLMADES

Distinctive dill and mint combine with the textures of currants and pine nuts in these stuffed vine leaves, whose flavours develop over time for a delicious make-ahead lunch.

MAKES 24 · PREP 30 MINS · COOK 1 HR

225g (8oz) jar of vine leaves, minimum 24 leaves

140g (5oz) cooked quinoa

1½ tbsp chopped mint leaves

1½ tbsp chopped dill

1½ tbsp chopped flat-leaf parsley

45g (1½oz) dried currants

30g (1oz) toasted pine nuts

2 tbsp olive oil

3 tbsp lemon juice

salt and freshly ground black pepper

300g (10oz) cooked moth beans, or black lentils

240ml (8fl oz) vegetable stock

1 Preheat the oven to 180°C (350°F). Lightly grease a 23 x 30cm (9 x 12in) glass or ceramic baking dish. Fill a large bowl with warm water. Soak the vine leaves for 2–3 minutes until pliable. Drain in a colander. Cover the colander with a wet towel, so they remain moist during assembly.

2 To make the filling, in a large mixing bowl combine the quinoa, mint, dill, parsley, currants, pine nuts, 1 tablespoon of oil, 1 tablespoon of lemon juice, and the cooked moth beans (or lentils). Season with salt and pepper.

3 To assemble the dolmades, place one vine leaf on a clean, flat work surface, vein-side up, and cut off the stem. Place 1 heaped tablespoon of filling in the centre, towards the bottom of the leaf. Fold the sides over the filling and roll tightly from stem to tip. Place seam-side down in the baking dish. Repeat with the remaining leaves, arranging snugly.

4 Pour the stock over the dolmades and drizzle over the remaining 1 tablespoon of oil and 2 tablespoons of lemon juice.

5 Cover the baking dish with foil and bake for 20–30 minutes until all the liquid has absorbed and the dolmades are moist and steaming. Serve immediately or leave to cool and store in an airtight container in the fridge for up to 2 days.

Make it with meat

Stir in 45g (1½oz) cooked minced lamb or beef with the quinoa filling.

Why not try...

For a tangier bite, sprinkle 45g (1½oz) of finely crumbled feta cheese into the quinoa filling before rolling the dolmades.

Nutrition per dolma

Calories	60
Total Fat	2.5g
Saturated Fat	0g
Cholesterol	0mg
Sodium	220mg
Total Carbohydrate	7g
Dietary Fibre	2g
Sugars	2g
Protein	2g

MASALA CHICKPEA NACHOS

This hybrid recipe combines the warm spices of Indian cuisine with the cheesy crunch of Tex-Mex nachos.

SERVES 6 · PREP 40 MINS · COOK 20 MINS

125g (4½oz) coriander leaves

30g (1oz) mint leaves

2 tbsp lemon juice

¼ tsp ground ginger

80ml (3fl oz) cold water

salt and freshly ground
  black pepper

350g (12oz) cooked chickpeas

1 tsp curry powder

1 tsp garam masala

1 tbsp vegetable oil

10 poppadoms, cooked
  according to instructions

225g (8oz) grated mozzarella
  cheese

125g (4½oz) mango chutney

30g (1oz) diced red onion

1 large lime, cut into
  6 wedges

1 To make the coriander-mint sauce, in a blender combine two-thirds of the coriander with the mint, lemon juice, ginger, and water. Purée until smooth. Season with salt and pepper. Transfer to an airtight container and set aside.

2 Preheat the oven to 200°C (400°F). Line a baking tray with foil. Toss the chickpeas with the curry powder, garam masala, and oil. Spread in an even layer on the baking tray and bake for 10 minutes, or until just crispy and warmed through. Transfer to a bowl and wipe the baking sheet.

3 Break each poppadom into quarters and arrange in a single layer on the baking tray. Sprinkle half the mozzarella over the poppadoms and top with the chickpea mixture. Then top with the remaining mozzarella and bake for 10–12 minutes, until the mozzarella melts and the poppadoms are lightly brown.

4 Meanwhile, in a small saucepan, heat the mango chutney with 1 tablespoon of water. Cook for 2–3 minutes until thin and warmed through.

5 To finish the assembly, sprinkle the onion over the melted cheese and drizzle mango chutney sauce over the top. Dollop the coriander-mint sauce across the nachos. Chop the remaining coriander and sprinkle over the nachos. Garnish with lime wedges and serve immediately, directly from the tray.

● Make it vegan

Use a soya mozzarella-style cheese alternative instead of mozzarella.

● Make it with meat

Add 125g (4½oz) cooked chopped chicken with the chickpeas in step 3.

Nutrition per serving

Calories	420
Total Fat	18g
Saturated Fat	12g
Cholesterol	40mg
Sodium	660mg
Total Carbohydrate	40g
Dietary Fibre	6g
Sugars	13g
Protein	26g

GARLIC ONION CHICKPEA FLOUR CRACKERS

Chickpea flour has a nutty flavour that goes well with these garlicky onion crackers, while crunchy seeds enhance the texture. Try them with your favourite dip.

MAKES 24 · PREP 30 MINS · COOK 15 MINS

½ tbsp sesame seeds
½ tbsp black sesame seeds
½ tbsp poppy seeds
½ tsp baking powder
115g (4oz) chickpea flour
¾ tsp salt
⅛ tsp onion powder
⅛ tsp garlic powder
2 tbsp olive oil
80ml (3fl oz) water

1 To make the topping, combine in a small bowl the sesame seeds, black sesame seeds, and poppy seeds. Set aside.

2 Preheat the oven to 190°C (375°F). Prepare a clean, flat work surface and cut two large pieces of baking parchment, each about 30 x 40cm (12 x 16in).

3 To make the dough, in a large mixing bowl combine the baking powder, chickpea flour, salt, onion powder, garlic powder, and oil. Gradually incorporate 60ml (2fl oz) water until a dough forms, adding additional water a spoonful at a time as needed, until the dough is just pliable. Place in the fridge to rest for 10 minutes.

4 Divide the dough into two pieces and place side by side between the two sheets of baking parchment, about 12cm (5in) apart. With a rolling pin, roll out as thinly as possible into 2 rectangles, about 3mm (⅛in) thick.

5 Remove the top sheet of baking parchment. With a pizza cutter or paring knife, score the dough into 3 x 3cm (1 x 1in) squares, making 24 crackers. Brush the dough with 1–2 teaspoons of water, then sprinkle the seed mixture evenly across the top.

6 Transfer the bottom piece of baking parchment directly onto a baking sheet. Bake for 10–15 minutes until the edges start to brown and the crackers are firm. Leave to rest at room temperature for 5 minutes, then break the crackers apart. Store in an airtight container for up to 3 days.

Nutrition per cracker

Calories	30
Total Fat	1.5g
Saturated Fat	0g
Cholesterol	0mg
Sodium	75mg
Total Carbohydrate	2g
Dietary Fibre	0g
Sugars	0g
Protein	1g

RED LENTIL CAPONATA

This Sicilian aubergine dish is often served as a dip or starter.

SERVES 6 · PREP 25 MINS · COOK 1 HR

1 large aubergine, diced

3 tbsp olive oil

1 onion, diced

2 garlic cloves, finely chopped

1 celery stick, chopped

2 large tomatoes, deseeded and chopped

3 tbsp capers

2 tbsp toasted pine nuts

30g (1oz) golden raisins

115g (4oz) cooked red lentils

1 tbsp sugar

80ml (3fl oz) red wine vinegar

pinch of crushed dried chillies

$1/8$ tsp cinnamon

$1/8$ tsp cocoa powder

1 Preheat the oven to 200°C (400°F). Spread the aubergine on a baking tray. Drizzle with 2 tablespoons of oil. Roast for 20 minutes, until tender.

2 In a large frying pan, heat the remaining 1 tablespoon of oil. Add the onion and cook for 2–3 minutes until soft. Add the garlic and cook for 1 minute. Add the celery, tomatoes, and aubergine, and cook for 5 minutes.

3 Add the capers, pine nuts, raisins, lentils, sugar, vinegar, crushed dried chillies, cinnamon, and cocoa powder. Simmer for 10 minutes, covered. Season with salt and freshly ground black pepper to taste. Remove from the heat and let cool. Refrigerate in an airtight container for 2 hours or overnight before serving.

Nutrition per serving

Calories	180	Sodium	500mg
Total Fat	11g	Total Carbohydrate	22g
Saturated Fat	1.5g	Dietary Fibre	6g
Cholesterol	0mg	Sugars	12g
		Protein	4g

RED PEPPER & WHITE BEAN DIP

This flavour-packed, 15-minute dip is the ultimate recipe for easy entertaining.

SERVES 8 · PREP 15 MINS

350g (12oz) cooked chickpeas

150g (5½oz) roasted red peppers, drained

325g (11oz) cooked cannellini beans

zest and juice of 1 lemon

1 tsp crushed dried chillies

1 tbsp thyme leaves

1 tbsp chopped flat-leaf parsley

1 tbsp olive oil

salt and pepper

1 In a food processor, add the chickpeas, roasted red peppers, cannellini beans, lemon zest and juice, crushed dried chillies, thyme, and parsley. Purée on low until well blended.

2 With the food processor running, drizzle in the oil. Season with salt and pepper to taste and pulse once more until the mixture is smooth but not runny. Serve immediately with pitta or crudités, or store in an airtight container in the fridge for up to 2 days.

Nutrition per serving

Calories	150	Sodium	400mg
Total Fat	3g	Total Carbohydrate	23g
Saturated Fat	0g	Dietary Fibre	7g
Cholesterol	0mg	Sugars	4g
		Protein	8g

GREEN SPLIT PEA & VEGETABLE DUMPLINGS

Steamed dumplings are a fun and interactive snack to make with friends and family. Pre-made wonton wrappers make this an easy dish to create.

MAKES 36 · PREP 35 MINS · COOK 1 HR 20 MINS

● **Make it with meat**

Add 125g (4½oz) cooked minced pork with the cabbage, and reduce the cabbage to 150g (5oz).

160ml (5fl oz) rice wine vinegar

160ml (5fl oz) soy sauce

½ tsp Sriracha

3 tbsp sesame oil

2 garlic cloves, finely chopped

1 tsp fresh grated ginger

3 spring onions, finely chopped

225g (8oz) finely shredded savoy cabbage

200g (7oz) cooked green split peas

pinch of crushed dried chillies

1 tsp mirin

15g (½oz) chopped coriander

1 tsp cornflour

1 tbsp water

36 x 8cm (3in) wonton wrappers

1 To make the dipping sauce, in a small bowl whisk together the rice wine vinegar, soy sauce, and Sriracha. Set aside.

2 To make the filling, in a large frying pan heat 1 tablespoon of sesame oil over a medium heat until warm. Add the garlic and ginger and cook for 1–2 minutes until soft. Then add the spring onion and cabbage and cook for 2–3 minutes until the cabbage begins to wilt. Add the split peas, crushed dried chillies, and mirin. Cook for 2–3 additional minutes until warmed through. Season with salt and freshly ground black pepper to taste. Stir in the coriander and remove from heat.

3 Prepare a clean, flat work surface to assemble the dumplings. In a small bowl, whisk together the cornflour and water. Place 1 wonton wrapper on the work surface and place 1 scant tablespoon of filling into the middle. Brush all four edges with the cornflour mixture. Fold the wrapper in half and press the edges together to seal, then set aside. Repeat with the remaining wrappers and filling.

4 In a non-stick frying pan, add 240ml (8fl oz) water, bring to the boil, then reduce to a gentle simmer. In another non-stick frying pan, heat the remaining 2 tablespoons of sesame oil over a medium-low heat until warm. Working in batches, fry the dumplings in the sesame oil for 2–3 minutes per side until golden brown. Then transfer the batch to the simmering water, cover, and steam for 2 minutes. Repeat with the remaining dumplings. Serve immediately with the soy dipping sauce.

Nutrition per dumpling

Calories	50
Total Fat	1.5g
Saturated Fat	0g
Cholesterol	0mg
Sodium	490mg
Total Carbohydrate	7g
Dietary Fibre	1g
Sugars	1g
Protein	2g

SOUPS
& STEWS

TOMATILLO SOUP
WITH HARICOT BEANS & CORN

Inspired by Mexican tortilla soup, this recipe gets texture from the sweetcorn and tang from the tomatillos. The creamy avocado and fresh coriander garnish make this dish extra special.

SERVES 10 · PREP 20 MINS · COOK 50 MINS

2 tbsp vegetable oil

1 onion, diced

2 large garlic cloves, finely chopped

1 jalapeño, deseeded and finely diced

pinch of crushed dried chillies

15 medium tomatillos, about 4cm (1½in) in diameter (or small, unripe tomatoes)

1.5 litres (2¾ pints) vegetable stock

kernels from 2 cobs of sweetcorn

800g (1¾lb) cooked haricot beans

juice of 2 large limes

10g (¼oz) chopped coriander leaves

salt and freshly ground black pepper

cubes of ripe avocado, to garnish

lime wedges, to garnish

1 In a large stock pot or saucepan, heat the oil over a medium heat until shimmering. Add the onion and cook for 3–4 minutes until translucent but not brown. Add the garlic, jalapeño, and crushed dried chillies, and cook for 2 minutes, or until soft.

2 Rinse the tomatillos, remove the husks, and roughly chop. Add to the pan and stir to combine. Cook for 7–8 minutes, covered, until the tomatillos begin to soften. Stir in the stock and bring to the boil. Reduce the heat and simmer, covered, for 20–25 minutes.

3 Stir in the sweetcorn, haricot beans, lime juice, and coriander. Cook for another 8–10 minutes until heated through. Season with salt and pepper to taste. To serve, ladle the soup into bowls and garnish with the avocado. Top each bowl with a lime wedge and serve immediately.

● **Make it with meat**

Add 140g (5oz) cooked chopped chicken when you stir in the sweetcorn and beans.

Why not try...

For a delightfully chewy texture, add 85g (3oz) Mexican pozole (hominy) with the corn, and reduce the haricot beans to 700g (1½lb).

Nutrition per serving

Calories	330
Total Fat	8g
Saturated Fat	1.5g
Cholesterol	0mg
Sodium	115mg
Total Carbohydrate	55g
Dietary Fibre	15g
Sugars	6g
Protein	11g

HOPPIN' JOHN SOUP

Traditionally served in the Southern US states on New Year's Day to bring good luck, Hoppin' John soup is usually a side dish, but here it's transformed into a hearty and healthy meal.

SERVES 6 · PREP 30 MINS · COOK 40 MINS

1 tbsp olive oil

1 small onion, diced

1 small red pepper, deseeded and diced

2 celery sticks, diced

1 garlic clove, finely chopped

400g (14oz) can chopped tomatoes

2 sprigs of thyme

pinch of ground cayenne pepper

½ tsp smoked paprika

1 litre (1¾ pints) vegetable stock

salt and freshly ground black pepper

375g (13oz) cooked black-eyed beans

175g (6oz) cooked brown rice

45g (1½oz) chopped spring onion

5g (¼oz) chopped flat-leaf parsley

1 In a large saucepan, warm the oil over a medium-low heat. Add the onion and cook for 2 minutes, or until it starts to become translucent. Add the red pepper and celery and cook for an additional 2 minutes. Add the garlic and cook for an additional minute.

2 Incorporate the tomatoes, thyme, cayenne, paprika, and stock. Bring to the boil, then reduce the heat to low and cook, covered, for 20 minutes. Season with salt and pepper to taste.

3 Combine the black-eyed beans and rice. Cook for an additional 10 minutes, or until the beans and rice are warmed through. Transfer to serving bowls and garnish with the spring onion and parsley.

Nutrition per serving

Calories	180
Total Fat	3g
Saturated Fat	0g
Cholesterol	0mg
Sodium	680mg
Total Carbohydrate	30g
Dietary Fibre	6g
Sugars	5g
Protein	6g

● **Make it with meat**

Stir in 140g (5oz) chopped, cooked, smoked turkey or ham when adding the stock and the tomatoes.

BUTTER BEAN BISQUE

The natural creaminess of butter beans gives this soup the texture of a bisque without the heaviness. Serve with home-made croutons and freshly ground black pepper.

SERVES 4 · PREP 15 MINS · COOK 30 MINS

1 tbsp unsalted butter

1 onion, chopped

2 celery sticks, chopped

600g (1lb 5oz) cooked butter beans

1.2 litres (2 pints) vegetable stock

½ tsp crushed dried chillies

4 sprigs of thyme

2 tbsp chopped basil leaves

2 tbsp chopped flat-leaf parsley

salt and freshly ground black pepper

1 In a large stock pot or saucepan, melt the butter over a medium heat. Add the onion and cook for 4–5 minutes until it starts to become translucent but not brown. Add the celery and cook for an additional 3–4 minutes until it starts to soften.

2 Add the butter beans and stir to combine. Pour in the stock and bring to the boil. Add the crushed dried chillies and thyme, then reduce the heat to a simmer. Cook, uncovered, for 15 minutes. Turn off the heat, remove the thyme stems, and stir in the basil and parsley. Leave to cool.

3 Once cool, working in batches, pour the soup into a blender and purée. Return to the pan and reheat. Season with salt and pepper to taste. Serve immediately.

Nutrition per serving

Calories	280
Total Fat	3.5g
Saturated Fat	2g
Cholesterol	10mg
Sodium	190mg
Total Carbohydrate	46g
Dietary Fibre	15g
Sugars	10g
Protein	15g

● **Make it with meat**

Garnish each bowl of soup with 1 tablespoon of crumbled crispy bacon or Parma ham.

GUMBO Z'HERBES

Also known as green gumbo, Gumbo Z'herbes is a longstanding tradition in Louisiana. Classically vegetarian, it is often eaten on Good Friday, and is thought to bring good luck all year long.

●Make it with meat

Add 140g (5oz) of chopped smoked turkey.

SERVES 10 · PREP 1 HR 10 MINS · COOK 1 HR

1 bunch Swiss chard

1 bunch kale

1 bunch watercress

1 bunch collard greens

1 bunch chicory

60g (2oz) baby spinach

400g (14oz) cooked moth beans, or black lentils

150ml (5fl oz) vegetable oil

100g (3½oz) plain flour

1 onion, diced

1 green pepper, diced

3 celery sticks, diced

1 garlic clove, finely chopped

500ml (16fl oz) vegetable stock

2 bay leaves

½ tsp paprika

3 sprigs of thyme

1 tsp ground cayenne pepper

2 tbsp white wine vinegar

salt and freshly ground black pepper

hot sauce (optional)

1 Remove and discard any tough stems and ribs from the greens and the spinach leaves. Roughly chop the greens – you want to end up with about 1kg (2lb). Place the greens in a large bowl and cover in cold water. Agitate to rinse out any dirt, then drain.

2 In a stock pot or large saucepan, bring 1.5 litres (2¾ pints) of water to a rapid boil. Add the greens and cook, covered, for 15–20 minutes, until tender. Reserve 500ml (16fl oz) of cooking liquid then drain the cooked greens.

3 In a blender or food processor, blend half the cooked greens, half the moth beans (or black lentils), and the reserved cooking liquid until smooth. Set aside.

4 To make a roux, in a large heavy-based saucepan or flameproof casserole, heat the oil over a medium heat. Once shimmering, add the flour and stir until smooth. Reduce the heat to low and stir continuously for 10–15 minutes until the roux is the colour of peanut butter and the consistency of milk.

5 Immediately stir in the onion, green pepper, and celery. Cook for 2–3 minutes over a medium heat, stirring continuously, until the mixture thickens and the vegetables are coated. Add the garlic, stock, bay leaves, paprika, thyme, and cayenne. Add the puréed greens and bean mixture and cook, covered, for 15 minutes.

6 Add the remaining cooked greens and moth beans (or lentils) and simmer briskly for 15 minutes, covered. Stir in the vinegar. Season with salt and pepper to taste. Remove the bay leaf and thyme stems and serve immediately, with hot sauce, if using.

Nutrition per serving

Calories	260
Total Fat	16g
Saturated Fat	10g
Cholesterol	0mg
Sodium	390mg
Total Carbohydrate	25g
Dietary Fibre	8g
Sugars	4g
Protein	8g

TOMATO & SPLIT PEA BISQUE

Smoky chipotle and tangy tomatoes flavour this creamy soup.

SERVES 6 · PREP 25 MINS · COOK 45 MINS

1 tbsp olive oil
1 onion, chopped
1 carrot, diced
1 celery stick, diced
1 garlic clove, crushed
400g (14oz) can chopped tomatoes
350g (12oz) cooked yellow split peas

1 chipotle in adobo (or rehydrated dried chipotle), finely chopped
750ml (1¼ pints) vegetable stock
1 tsp ground coriander
juice of 1 lime
90ml (3fl oz) double cream
salt and pepper

1 In a medium stock pot or flameproof casserole, heat the oil over a medium-low heat until shimmering. Add the onion, carrot, and celery and cook for 2–3 minutes. Add the garlic and cook for 1–2 minutes.

2 Add the tomatoes, split peas, chipotle, stock, and coriander. Stir to combine. Bring to the boil, then reduce to a simmer and cook, covered, for 20–25 minutes until the soup thickens. Remove from the heat and let cool for 5–10 minutes.

3 In a blender, working in batches, purée the soup until completely smooth. Return to the pan and reheat. Stir in the lime juice and cream. Season with salt and pepper to taste. Serve immediately.

Nutrition per serving

Calories	230
Total Fat	8g
Saturated Fat	3.5g
Cholesterol	20mg
Sodium	380mg
Total Carbohydrate	32g
Dietary Fibre	11g
Sugars	8g
Protein	9g

● **Make it vegan**

Instead of double cream, use an equal amount of coconut cream.

LEMON & HERB SPLIT PEA SOUP

This classic soup is lightened with fresh flavours of citrus, thyme, and basil.

SERVES 6 · PREP 20 MINS · COOK 1 HR 10 MINS

1 tbsp olive oil
1 onion, chopped
1 carrot, diced
1 large celery stick, diced
1 garlic clove, finely chopped
350g (12oz) uncooked split green peas
1.5 litres (2½ pints) vegetable stock

pinch of crushed dried chillies
3 sprigs of thyme
½ tbsp chopped basil leaves
zest and juice of 2 large lemons
salt and pepper

1 In a stock pot, heat the oil over a medium-low heat until shimmering. Add the onion, carrot, and celery and cook for 2–3 minutes until soft. Add the garlic and cook for an additional minute.

2 Add the split peas, stock, crushed dried chillies, and thyme. Bring to the boil, then reduce heat and simmer, covered, for 45 minutes to 1 hour, stirring frequently, until the split peas are tender and the soup thickens.

3 Stir in the basil and lemon zest and juice. Season with salt and pepper to taste. Remove the thyme stems and serve immediately.

Nutrition per serving

Calories	200
Total Fat	2.5g
Saturated Fat	0g
Cholesterol	0mg
Sodium	560mg
Total Carbohydrate	42g
Dietary Fibre	17g
Sugars	5g
Protein	15g

● **Make it with meat**

For a smoky complement, add 2 chopped bacon rashers and cook with the onion.

KABOCHA SQUASH & YELLOW LENTIL SOUP

Kabocha is a winter squash with a sweet flavour and vivid orange flesh. Roasting enhances its sweetness, making it a natural companion to curry and coconut milk.

SERVES 4 · PREP 20 MINS · COOK 1 HR 40 MINS

1 kabocha squash
  (or butternut squash),
  deseeded and cut
  into quarters

2 tbsp olive oil

1 carrot, chopped

1 onion, chopped

1 celery stick, chopped

1.25 litres (2 pints) vegetable
  stock

325g (11oz) uncooked
  yellow lentils

2 tsp curry powder

½ tsp ground ginger

small can (165ml; 5.6fl oz)
  unsweetened coconut milk

salt and freshly ground
  black pepper

1 lime, cut into 4 wedges

unsweetened, toasted
  coconut flakes, to garnish

1 Preheat the oven to 180°C (350°F). Place the squash quarters cut-side up on a baking tray and drizzle with 1 tablespoon of oil. Roast for 40 minutes, or until tender. Leave to cool.

2 Meanwhile, in a large saucepan, heat the remaining 1 tablespoon oil over a medium heat. Add the carrot, onion, and celery and cook for 3 minutes, or until translucent. Add 750ml (1¼ pints) of stock and the yellow lentils and bring to the boil. Reduce to a simmer and cook, covered, for 45 minutes to 1 hour, until the lentils are tender. To ensure there is enough liquid for the lentils to absorb, add up to 500ml (15fl oz) of additional stock as needed.

3 When the lentils are tender, scoop the roasted kabocha from its skin and add the flesh to the pan. Stir in the curry powder and ginger and heat through. With a blender or hand-held blender, purée until smooth. Stir in the coconut milk and heat thoroughly. Season with salt and pepper to taste. Serve with a lime wedge.

● **Make it with meat**

Use chicken stock rather than vegetable stock and garnish each serving with ½ rasher of crumbled crispy bacon.

Nutrition per serving

Calories	322
Total Fat	15g
Saturated Fat	8g
Cholesterol	0mg
Sodium	287mg
Total Carbohydrate	41g
Dietary Fibre	13g
Sugars	4g
Protein	8g

Pulse exchange
In place of the yellow lentils, substitute an equal amount of **red lentils**.

MUNG BEAN & MISO NOODLE SOUP

This comforting Asian soup gets an extra layer of texture and a boost of protein from the addition of mung beans.

SERVES 6 · PREP 15 MINS · COOK 15 MINS

1.25 litres (2 pints) vegetable stock

3 tbsp white miso paste

1 tbsp fresh grated ginger

2 garlic cloves, finely chopped

2 tbsp rice wine vinegar

2 tsp soy sauce

85g (3oz) uncooked Japanese udon noodles

250g (9oz) cooked mung beans

200g (7oz) extra firm tofu, drained, pressed, and diced

140g (5oz) shredded Savoy cabbage

45g (1½ oz) sliced spring onion, to garnish

1 In a medium flameproof casserole or stock pot, combine the stock, miso paste, ginger, garlic, vinegar, and soy sauce.

2 Bring the mixture to the boil and add the udon noodles. Reduce the heat and simmer for 5–6 minutes until the noodles start to become tender.

3 Add the mung beans, tofu, and cabbage. Stir to combine thoroughly and cook for 5 minutes, or until the udon are completely cooked and the tofu is warmed through.

4 Transfer to serving bowls and garnish with the spring onion. Serve immediately.

Nutrition per serving

Calories	160
Total Fat	3g
Saturated Fat	0g
Cholesterol	0mg
Sodium	630mg
Total Carbohydrate	24g
Dietary Fibre	6g
Sugars	5g
Protein	11g

● **Make it with meat**

For a seafood version, add 225g (8oz) cooked, peeled prawns to the soup, along with the mung beans.

GREEN MINESTRONE
WITH ROCKET PESTO

This version of the classic Italian soup uses the fresh, green produce of spring, and is topped off with a dollop of vibrant home-made pesto.

SERVES 6 · PREP 50 MINS · COOK 40 MINS

135ml (4½fl oz) olive oil

1 large trimmed leek, sliced

1 large celery stick, diced

1 garlic clove, finely chopped

1.25 litres (2 pints) vegetable stock

1 bay leaf

1 sprig of thyme

pinch of crushed dried chillies

450g (1lb) cooked haricot beans

1 small courgette, diced

125g (4½oz) trimmed green beans, cut into 3cm (1in) pieces

1 tbsp chopped basil leaves

115g (4oz) frozen peas, thawed

85g (3oz) shredded Savoy cabbage

½ tsp chopped oregano

20g (¾oz) baby rocket

60g (2oz) pine nuts, toasted

125g (4½oz) grated Parmesan cheese

1 tsp grated lemon zest

1 In a medium stock pot, heat 1 tablespoon of oil over a medium-low heat. Add the leek and cook for 2–3 minutes until it begins to soften. Add the celery and garlic and cook for an additional 2–3 minutes.

2 Add the stock, bay leaf, thyme, crushed dried chillies, and haricot beans. Bring to the boil then reduce the heat and simmer, covered, for 15 minutes, or until the haricot beans are warmed through.

3 Add the courgette, green beans, basil, peas, Savoy cabbage, and oregano. Simmer for an additional 15 minutes, or until the vegetables are tender and cooked through. Season with salt and pepper to taste.

4 Meanwhile, to make the pesto, in a food processor combine the rocket, pine nuts, Parmesan, and lemon zest. With the processor running, slowly drizzle in the remaining 120ml (4fl oz) of oil until fully combined.

5 Remove the bay leaf. Divide the soup among 6 bowls and top each with ½ tablespoon pesto. Serve immediately.

● **Make it with meat**

Add 140g (5oz) cooked, diced chicken along with the vegetables in step 3, and use chicken stock in place of vegetable stock.

Nutrition per serving

Calories	390
Total Fat	20g
Saturated Fat	5g
Cholesterol	10mg
Sodium	410mg
Total Carbohydrate	30g
Dietary Fibre	11g
Sugars	5g
Protein	15g

Pulse exchange

Substitute an equal amount of **mung beans** or **cannellini beans** for the haricot beans.

CARIBBEAN BLACK BEAN & LENTIL SOUP

Peppers and jalapeño flavour this comforting and slightly spicy soup, made heartier with black beans and beluga lentils.

SERVES 4 · PREP 25 MINS · COOK 30 MINS

1 tbsp vegetable oil

115g (4oz) onion, diced

75g (2½oz) red pepper, diced

75g (2½oz) green pepper, diced

1 small jalapeño, deseeded and finely chopped

1 tbsp garlic, finely chopped

1 litre (1¾ pints) vegetable stock

1 bay leaf

350g (12oz) uncooked black beans, soaked

150g (5½oz) cooked beluga lentils

1½ tsp allspice

¼ tsp ground cayenne pepper

½ tsp smoked paprika

juice of 2 limes

salt and freshly ground black pepper

chopped coriander, to garnish

1 In a medium stock pot or flameproof casserole, heat the oil over a medium heat. Add the onion, green and red peppers, and jalapeño. Cook for 4–5 minutes until the vegetables begin to soften. Add the garlic and cook for an additional 1–2 minutes.

2 Incorporate the stock, bay leaf, black beans, beluga lentils, allspice, cayenne, and paprika. Bring to the boil then reduce the heat and simmer, covered, for 20 minutes, or until the soup begins to thicken.

3 Stir in the lime juice. Season with salt and pepper to taste. Remove the bay leaf and garnish with the coriander before serving.

● **Make it with meat**

For a tasty complement, add 1 cooked, smoked sausage (about 85–110g; 3–4oz) along with the vegetables in step 1.

Nutrition per serving

Calories	400
Total Fat	7g
Saturated Fat	3g
Cholesterol	0mg
Sodium	150mg
Total Carbohydrate	68g
Dietary Fibre	17g
Sugars	7g
Protein	21g

Pulse exchange

Substitute an equal amount of **adzuki beans** for the black beans.

YELLOW LENTIL MULLIGATAWNY

This spicy and sweet lentil soup is an Anglo-Indian classic.

SERVES 8 · PREP 25 MINS · COOK 45 MINS

2 tbsp coconut oil

1 onion, diced

2 celery sticks, diced

2 carrots, diced

3 garlic cloves, finely chopped

¾ tsp curry powder

¾ tsp ground coriander

¼ tsp ground cayenne pepper

200g (7oz) uncooked yellow lentils

400g (14oz) can chopped tomatoes

1 litre (1¾ pints) vegetable stock

400ml (14fl oz) can coconut milk

juice of 2 large limes

chopped coriander leaves, to garnish

1 In a stock pot, heat the coconut oil over a medium-low heat. Add the onion, celery, and carrots and cook for 2–3 minutes until soft. Add the garlic and cook for an additional minute.

2 Add the curry powder, ground coriander, and cayenne. Cook 1 minute then stir in the lentils. Add the tomatoes, stock, and coconut milk. Bring to the boil, reduce to a simmer and cook, covered, for 20–35 minutes until the lentils are tender.

3 Stir in the lime juice. Season with salt and pepper to taste. Transfer to serving bowls, garnish with coriander, and serve immediately.

Nutrition per serving

Calories	200
Total Fat	9g
Saturated Fat	7g
Cholesterol	0mg
Sodium	190mg
Total Carbohydrate	24g
Dietary Fibre	6g
Sugars	6g
Protein	7g

● **Make it with meat**

For a stronger flavour, use chicken stock in place of the vegetable stock.

SPICY RED LENTIL SOUP

In this soup, the heat of chillies is balanced by smoky paprika and earthy cumin.

SERVES 4 · PREP 25 MINUTES · COOK 40 MINUTES

1 tbsp olive oil

1 large carrot, peeled and diced

1 onion, diced

1 small green Thai chilli or jalapeño, finely diced

175g (6oz) uncooked red lentils

750ml (1¼ pints) water

1 tbsp tomato purée

400g (14oz) can chopped tomatoes

1 tbsp smoked paprika

2 tsp light brown sugar

2½ tsp ground cumin

1 tsp Sriracha

salt and freshly ground black pepper

chopped spring onions, to garnish

1 In a large stock pot, heat the oil over a medium heat until shimmering. Add the carrot and onion and cook for 4–5 minutes until soft. Add the chilli and cook for another 1–2 minutes. Stir in the lentils.

2 Add the water, tomato purée, chopped tomatoes, paprika, sugar, cumin, and Sriracha. Bring to the boil then reduce the heat and simmer, covered, for 35–40 minutes, until the vegetables and lentils are cooked.

3 Season with salt and pepper to taste. Transfer to serving bowls and garnish with the spring onions. Serve immediately.

Nutrition per serving

Calories	240
Total Fat	3.5g
Saturated Fat	0.5g
Cholesterol	0mg
Sodium	260mg
Total Carbohydrate	40g
Dietary Fibre	10g
Sugars	9g
Protein	13g

● **Make it with meat**

For a smoky complement, add 2 rashers of bacon and sauté with the carrot and onion.

PIGEON PEA & PUMPKIN CHILLI

Pumpkin may seem like an unusual ingredient in chilli, but its sweetness is a lovely complement to the spiciness of this soup.

SERVES 6 · PREP 25 MINS · COOK 45 MINS

1 tbsp olive oil

1 small onion, diced

2 garlic cloves, finely chopped

1 small jalapeño, deseeded and minced

400g (14oz) can chopped tomatoes

2½ tsp ground cumin

1½ tsp chipotle chilli powder

500ml (16fl oz) vegetable stock

375g (13oz) cooked pigeon peas, or black-eyed beans

400g (14oz) cooked adzuki beans

115g (4oz) sweetcorn kernels

425g (15oz) can pure pumpkin

salt and freshly ground black pepper

60g (2oz) chopped coriander leaves, to garnish

1 In a large stock pot, heat the oil over a medium-low heat. Add the onion and cook for 2–3 minutes until soft. Add the garlic and jalapeño and cook for an additional minute.

2 Incorporate the tomatoes, cumin, and chipotle chilli powder. Stir in the stock, bring to the boil, reduce the heat and then simmer for 5 minutes. Stir in the pigeon peas (or black-eyed beans), adzuki beans, and sweetcorn. Return to the boil then reduce the heat to low and simmer, covered, for 20 minutes.

3 Fold in the pumpkin and stir to combine. Cook, covered, for another 10 minutes. Season with salt and pepper to taste. Transfer to 6 serving bowls, garnish with the chopped coriander, and serve immediately.

Nutrition per serving

Calories	360
Total Fat	4g
Saturated Fat	0.5g
Cholesterol	0mg
Sodium	180mg
Total Carbohydrate	68g
Dietary Fibre	16g
Sugars	9g
Protein	15g

● **Make it with meat**

Cook 225g (8oz) raw turkey mince along with the onion in step 1.

CHICKPEA & HARICOT BEAN BISQUE

While not a traditional bisque, this soup certainly seems like one with its silky, rich texture. This simple, elegant recipe makes an excellent first course for a dinner party.

SERVES 4 · PREP 15 MINS · COOK 30 MINS

½ tbsp olive oil, plus extra to garnish

1 leek, white parts only, sliced

1 garlic clove, finely chopped

1 tbsp dry vermouth

750ml (1¼ pints) vegetable stock

450g (1lb) cooked haricot beans

175g (6oz) cooked chickpeas

60ml (2fl oz) double cream

salt and freshly ground black pepper

chopped toasted hazelnuts, to garnish

1 In a flameproof casserole or large saucepan, warm the oil over a medium-low heat until shimmering. Add the leek and cook for 4–5 minutes until soft and translucent. Add the garlic and cook for an additional 2 minutes.

2 Add the vermouth and cook for 1–2 minutes. Incorporate the stock, haricot beans, and chickpeas. Bring to the boil, then reduce to a simmer and cook, covered, for 15 minutes. Remove from the heat and leave to cool for 5–10 minutes.

3 Transfer the mixture to a blender and purée until smooth. Return to the pan over a medium heat, stir in the cream, and heat. Season with salt and pepper to taste. Transfer to serving bowls, garnish with the hazelnuts and a swirl of oil, and serve immediately.

Nutrition per serving

Calories	270
Total Fat	6g
Saturated Fat	2g
Cholesterol	10mg
Sodium	390mg
Total Carbohydrate	41g
Dietary Fibre	14g
Sugars	5g
Protein	12g

● **Make it vegan**

The cooked chickpeas are naturally creamy, so you can easily omit the double cream for a vegan-friendly version.

PIGEON PEA, QUINOA & KALE SOUP

This soup is hearty and filling without being heavy. It's also a nutritional powerhouse, with a trifecta of superfood ingredients providing vitamins, fibre, and protein.

SERVES 4 · PREP 25 MINS · COOK 45 MINS

1 tbsp olive oil

1 small onion, diced

1 large carrot, diced

1 celery stick, diced

1 garlic clove, finely chopped

pinch of crushed dried chillies

leaves from 3 sprigs of thyme

1 bay leaf

1.7 litres (3 pints) vegetable stock

400g (14oz) can chopped tomatoes

175g (6oz) uncooked red, white, and black quinoa

325g (11oz) cooked pigeon peas, or black-eyed beans

140g (5oz) chopped kale

salt and freshly ground black pepper

1 In a large flameproof casserole or saucepan, warm the oil over medium heat until shimmering. Add the onion, carrot, and celery and cook for 4 minutes, or until tender but not brown. Add the garlic and cook for an additional 2 minutes.

2 Add the crushed dried chillies, thyme, and bay leaf. Stir to combine, and cook for 1 minute. Add the stock and tomatoes. Bring to the boil, then add the quinoa. Reduce the heat to low and cook, partially covered, for 25 minutes, or until the quinoa is fully cooked.

3 Stir in the pigeon peas (or black-eyed beans) and kale. Cook for an additional 10 minutes, or until the kale is tender. Season with salt and pepper to taste. Remove the bay leaf and serve immediately.

Nutrition per serving

Calories	380
Total Fat	7g
Saturated Fat	0.5g
Cholesterol	0mg
Sodium	740mg
Total Carbohydrate	67g
Dietary Fibre	15g
Sugars	14g
Protein	15g

●Make it with meat

Remove the casings from 2 Italian sausages, crumble the meat, and add along with the garlic.

SOUTHWEST HARICOT SOUP

This soup has the vivid flavours of chilli, lime, and coriander, and a light, brothy texture.

SERVES 6 · PREP 10 MINS · COOK 1 HR 10 MINS

1 tbsp olive oil

1 onion, diced

1 small jalapeño, deseeded and diced

1 garlic clove, finely chopped

1 litre (1¾ pints) vegetable stock

1 tsp ground cumin

1 tsp smoked paprika

1 tsp dried oregano leaves

1 tsp ancho chilli powder

450g (1lb) soaked haricot beans

juice of 1 lime

1 tbsp chopped coriander

salt and pepper

1 In a large saucepan, heat the oil over a medium-low heat. Add the onion and jalapeño and cook for 2–3 minutes. Add the garlic and cook another 1–2 minutes.

2 Add the stock, cumin, paprika, oregano, and chilli powder. Add the haricot beans and stir to combine. Bring to the boil then reduce the heat and simmer, covered, for 45 minutes to 1 hour, until the beans are completely tender.

3 In a blender, purée 180ml (6fl oz) soup until smooth. Return to the pan and stir to combine.

4 Stir in the lime juice and coriander. Season with salt and pepper to taste. Serve immediately.

Nutrition per serving

Calories	280
Total Fat	3.5g
Saturated Fat	0g
Cholesterol	0mg
Sodium	290mg
Total Carbohydrate	47g
Dietary Fibre	18g
Sugars	5g
Protein	16g

● **Make it with meat**

Ham complements haricot beans. Add 60g (2oz) chopped cooked ham along with the beans.

FEIJOADA

This simple Brazilian stew, often a celebratory dish, is prepared at weekends when there is time to cook it very slowly.

SERVES 4 · PREP 20 MINS · COOK 1 HR

1 tbsp olive oil

1 red onion, chopped

1 celery stick, chopped

1 red or yellow pepper, deseeded and chopped

4 garlic cloves, finely chopped

2 sprigs of thyme

2 large tomatoes, deseeded and chopped

500g (1lb 2oz) cooked black beans

750ml (1¼ pints) vegetable stock

1 chipotle in adobo (or rehydrated dried chipotle), finely chopped

juice of 1 lime

salt and pepper

5g (¼oz) chopped parsley, to garnish

1 In a medium stock pot, heat the oil over a medium-high heat. Add the onion, celery, and red or yellow pepper. Cook, partially covered, for 5–6 minutes until soft. Add the garlic and cook for an additional 1–2 minutes.

2 Stir in the thyme, tomatoes, black beans, stock, and chipotle. Bring to the boil then reduce the heat and simmer, covered, for 45 minutes, stirring occasionally.

3 Remove from the heat and stir in the lime juice. Season with salt and pepper to taste. Garnish with parsley and serve immediately.

Nutrition per serving

Calories	280
Total Fat	5g
Saturated Fat	0.5g
Cholesterol	0mg
Sodium	580mg
Total Carbohydrate	45g
Dietary Fibre	16g
Sugars	10g
Protein	14g

● **Make it with meat**

For a more traditional Feijoada, add 1 chopped, cooked smoked sausage (85–110g; 3–4oz) with the beans in step 2.

MUNG BEAN GREEN GAZPACHO

Green gazpacho is a unique spin on the classic Spanish cold soup. It's best served ice cold, so don't skimp on the chilling time.

SERVES 4 · PREP 30 MINS

45g (1½oz) rocket leaves

1 cucumber, peeled, deseeded, and chopped

1 garlic clove

125g (4½oz) cooked mung beans

10g (¼oz) roughly chopped coriander leaves

10g (¼oz) mint leaves

3 spring onions, trimmed and chopped

1 avocado, halved and pitted

1 tbsp olive oil

2 tsp red wine vinegar

juice of 1 large lemon

300ml (10fl oz) cold water

salt and freshly ground black pepper

2 tbsp chopped chives

15g (½oz) sprouted mung beans (beansprouts)

1 In a food processor, combine the rocket, cucumber, garlic, mung beans, coriander, mint, and spring onion. Process on high until finely chopped.

2 Add the avocado, oil, vinegar, and lemon juice. Process on high while slowly incorporating the cold water. Season with salt and pepper to taste, and pulse once more to combine.

3 Transfer to an airtight container and refrigerate for at least 2 hours. Divide the gazpacho among 4 serving bowls and garnish with the chives and beansprouts.

● **Make it with meat**
Sauté 450g (1lb) peeled and de-veined king prawns with garlic, and add atop each serving.

Nutrition per serving

Calories	180
Total Fat	12g
Saturated Fat	2g
Cholesterol	0mg
Sodium	580mg
Total Carbohydrate	17g
Dietary Fibre	8g
Sugars	5g
Protein	6g

Why not try...
Garnish each serving with 1 tablespoon of diced, ripe avocado and a drizzle of extra virgin olive oil.

CREAMY SPINACH & MUNG BEAN SOUP

Don't let the bright colour fool you – this soup is as luxurious as it is good for you, and especially tasty with freshly baked bread.

SERVES 4 · PREP 25 MINS · COOK 40 MINS

1 tbsp unsalted butter

1 onion, diced

1 garlic clove, finely chopped

1 potato, peeled and cut into 1cm (½in) chunks

750ml (1¼ pints) vegetable stock

175g (6oz) baby spinach

175g (6oz) cooked mung beans

2 tbsp dry sherry

⅛ tsp ground cayenne pepper

⅛ tsp ground nutmeg

salt and freshly ground black pepper

20g (¾oz) grated Parmesan cheese

1 In a flameproof casserole or stock pot, melt the butter over a medium heat. Add the onion and cook for 3–4 minutes until translucent. Add the garlic and cook for 2 minutes.

2 Add the potato and stir to combine. Cook for 2–3 minutes. Add 500ml (16fl oz) stock and bring to the boil. Reduce the heat to a simmer and cook, covered, for 12–15 minutes, until the potatoes are tender.

3 Add the spinach and mung beans and cook for an additional 5 minutes, or until the spinach wilts and the mung beans are warmed through. Leave to cool.

4 With a blender (working in batches) or a hand-held blender, purée the soup until smooth. Return the puréed mixture to the pan and stir in the sherry, cayenne, and nutmeg. For a thinner consistency, add some of the remaining stock as desired. Season with salt and pepper to taste.

5 Reheat the soup over a medium heat. Transfer to serving bowls and top with Parmesan. Serve immediately.

● Make it vegan

Replace the butter with an equal amount of coconut oil.

● Make it with meat

Crumble 1 tablespoon of crisped Parma ham on top of each bowl of soup.

Nutrition per serving

Calories	180
Total Fat	5g
Saturated Fat	3g
Cholesterol	15mg
Sodium	800mg
Total Carbohydrate	25g
Dietary Fibre	6g
Sugars	4g
Protein	8g

Why not try...
Garnish with flat-leaf parsley or watercress for a more pronounced green flavour.

PINTO BEAN PEANUT STEW

Peanut soups and stews are a staple in parts of Africa. This unusual dish combines peanut butter with beans and bitter greens for a hearty stew.

SERVES 6 · PREP 25 MINS · COOK 45 MINS

1 tbsp coconut oil

1 small onion, chopped

1 garlic clove, finely chopped

1 large sweet potato, peeled and cut into 3cm (1in) cubes

1 tsp ancho chilli powder

½ tsp ground cayenne pepper

400g (14oz) can chopped tomatoes

600ml (1 pint) vegetable stock

125g (4½oz) smooth peanut butter

450g (1lb) cooked pinto beans

45g (1½oz) chopped leafy greens

salt and freshly ground black pepper

chopped coriander leaves, to garnish

1 In a medium stock pot, heat the coconut oil over a medium-low heat until shimmering. Add the onion and cook for 2–3 minutes until soft. Add the garlic and cook for 1 minute.

2 Add the sweet potato, ancho chilli powder, and cayenne. Stir to combine. Pour in the chopped tomatoes and stock. Bring to the boil then reduce to a simmer and cook, uncovered, for 5 minutes.

3 Stir in the peanut butter. Return to the boil then reduce the heat and simmer, covered, for 10 minutes.

4 Fold in the pinto beans and greens. Return to the boil once more, then reduce to a simmer and cook, covered, for 15 minutes, or until the greens are tender. Season with salt and pepper to taste. Garnish with the coriander and serve immediately.

● **Make it with meat**

Add 200g (7oz) raw, smoked andouille sausage, diced, along with the onion in step 1.

Nutrition per serving	
Calories	330
Total Fat	14g
Saturated Fat	4.5g
Cholesterol	0mg
Sodium	220mg
Total Carbohydrate	40g
Dietary Fibre	13g
Sugars	8g
Protein	16g

Pulse exchange

Instead of pinto beans, substitute an equal amount of **borlotti beans** or **black beans**.

SALADS & SIDES

THREE BEAN SALAD STUFFED AVOCADOS

These stuffed avocados are filled with the Southwestern flavours of sweetcorn and coriander. The three beans mean plenty of protein, while the avocado is a wonderful source of healthy fats.

SERVES 8 · PREP 20 MINS · COOK 15 MINS

1 corn on the cob

85g (3oz) cooked black beans

75g (2½ oz) cooked pigeon peas, or black-eyed beans

85g (3oz) cooked mung beans or 30g (1oz) sprouted mung beans

85g (3oz) cooked farro

1 orange or yellow pepper, diced

3 tbsp soured cream

¼ tsp smoked paprika

½ tsp ground cumin

1 tsp red wine vinegar

juice of 2 medium limes

1 tbsp olive oil

salt and freshly ground black pepper

4 ripe avocados

15g (½oz) chopped coriander leaves

1 Using a ridged cast-iron grill pan or a gas burner, char the corn on the cob for 1–2 minutes per side until slightly blackened. Let cool slightly.

2 Meanwhile, in a large mixing bowl, combine the black beans, pigeon peas (or black-eyed beans), mung beans, farro, and pepper. Carefully slice the kernels from the cob and add to the bowl.

3 To make the dressing, in a small bowl whisk together the soured cream, paprika, cumin, vinegar, and lime juice. Drizzle in the olive oil and whisk to combine thoroughly.

4 Pour the dressing over the bean mixture and toss to coat. Season with salt and pepper to taste.

5 Cut each avocado in half lengthways and remove the stones. Mound an equal amount of bean mixture into the centre of each. Place on serving plates and garnish with coriander.

Nutrition per serving

Calories	310
Total Fat	18g
Saturated Fat	3.5g
Cholesterol	0mg
Sodium	300mg
Total Carbohydrate	34g
Dietary Fibre	12g
Sugars	5g
Protein	8g

● Make it with meat

Fold 70g (2½oz) chopped, chargrilled chicken into the bean mixture in step 2.

BLACK LENTIL & KALE SALAD
WITH MISO TAHINI DRESSING

Loaded with texture, this salad is unlike most green salads. The chewy kale, crunchy coconut, creamy beans, and tangy dressing are a dynamic combination.

SERVES 6 · PREP 35 MINS

3 tbsp tahini

1½ tbsp miso paste

juice of 1 large lime

1 tsp soy sauce

2 tsp honey

2 tbsp rice wine vinegar

¼ tsp crushed dried chillies

60ml (2fl oz) cold water

1 bunch kale, tough stems removed and chopped, about 175g (6oz)

50g (1¾oz) unsweetened, coconut flakes

175g (6oz) cooked black lentils

salt and freshly ground black pepper

1 In a small non-stick frying pan, toast the coconut flakes over a medium-low heat for 4–5 minutes until light golden brown. Immediately remove from the heat and leave to cool completely.

2 To make the dressing, in a small mixing bowl, combine the tahini, miso paste, lime juice, soy sauce, honey, rice wine vinegar, and chillies. Add the water and whisk until smooth.

3 In a large salad bowl, add the chopped kale and about 180ml (6fl oz) of the dressing. With your hands, massage the dressing into the kale for 1–2 minutes until the kale tenderizes slightly.

4 Add the toasted coconut and black lentils and toss to combine. Season with salt and pepper to taste. Serve immediately.

● **Make it with meat**

To transform this salad into a meaty main course, add 85g (3oz) cooked, sliced chicken breast to each portion.

Nutrition per serving

Calories	210
Total Fat	13g
Saturated Fat	8g
Cholesterol	0mg
Sodium	370mg
Total Carbohydrate	19g
Dietary Fibre	7g
Sugars	5g
Protein	8g

Pulse exchange
Use an equal amount of **moth beans** instead of the black lentils.

ROASTED TENDERSTEM BROCCOLI & GREEN LENTIL SALAD

Roasting tenderstem broccoli highlights its best qualities – a bittersweet flavour and great texture.

SERVES 6 · PREP 20 MINS · COOK 15 MINS

juice of 1 large lemon
1 tsp thyme leaves
2 tbsp lemon zest
1 tbsp Dijon mustard
1 tbsp honey
175ml (5½fl oz) olive oil
450g (1lb) tenderstem broccoli
1 garlic clove, finely chopped
¼ tsp crushed dried chillies
salt and freshly ground black pepper
325g (11oz) cooked green or Puy lentils

1 To make the dressing, in a small bowl, mix together the lemon juice, thyme, 1 tablespoon lemon zest, Dijon mustard, honey, and 160ml (5fl oz) oil. Whisk until completely emulsified, and set aside.

2 Preheat the oven to 180°C (350°F). Trim the woody ends from the tenderstem broccoli, and cut each floret into 2–4 bite-sized pieces.

3 On a baking tray, toss the tenderstem broccoli, garlic, chillies, remaining 1 tablespoon lemon zest, and remaining 1 tablespoon olive oil. Spread out in an even layer and roast for 10–15 minutes until the broccoli is tender and slightly charred.

4 In a medium mixing bowl, toss the lentils and dressing. On a serving platter, spread the lentils in an even layer and top with the roasted tenderstem broccoli. Season with salt and pepper to taste. Serve immediately.

● Make it with meat

For a wonderful, salty garnish, sprinkle with with 3 tablespoons of crisped, crumbled Parma ham.

Why not try... Instead of tenderstem broccoli, use regular broccoli florets. Roast for 20 minutes, or until tender and slightly charred.

Nutrition per serving

Calories	150
Total Fat	0g
Saturated Fat	0g
Cholesterol	0mg
Sodium	360mg
Total Carbohydrate	27g
Dietary Fibre	9g
Sugars	8g
Protein	11g

ROASTED CARROTS & CHICKPEAS
WITH VADOUVAN YOGURT

Vadouvan, or French masala, is a curry spice blend originating from Southern India. Cool yogurt tempers the spice and pairs well with the sweetness of roasted carrots.

SERVES 4 · PREP 15 MINS · COOK 30 MINS

450g (1lb) whole young carrots, leafy tops chopped and reserved for garnish

2 tbsp olive oil

350g (12oz) cooked chickpeas

2 tsp red wine vinegar

1 garlic clove, finely chopped

1 tsp thyme leaves

pinch of crushed dried chillies

salt and freshly ground black pepper

150g (5½oz) plain Greek-style yogurt

1 tbsp vadouvan (French masala)

1 Preheat the oven to 150°C (350°F). Arrange the carrots in a single layer on a baking tray and drizzle with olive oil. Roast for 25–30 minutes until tender.

2 Meanwhile, in a small mixing bowl, toss together the chickpeas, vinegar, garlic, thyme, and crushed dried chillies. Season with salt and pepper. Set aside.

3 In another small mixing bowl, stir together the Greek-style yogurt and vadouvan.

4 Spread the yogurt on a serving plate, arrange the roasted carrots over the yogurt, and top with the chickpea mixture. Garnish with ground pepper and the reserved carrot leaves. Serve immediately.

Nutrition per serving

Calories	270
Total Fat	9g
Saturated Fat	1.5g
Cholesterol	<5mg
Sodium	230mg
Total Carbohydrate	37g
Dietary Fibre	7g
Sugars	12g
Protein	11g

●Make it vegan

Substitute an equal amount of plain soya yogurt for the Greek-style yogurt.

LENTIL & CAULIFLOWER TABBOULEH

Using cauliflower to make "grains" is an easy hack that adds nutrition without sacrificing flavour. Here, cauliflower combines beautifully with fresh mint and herbs in this Middle Eastern salad.

SERVES 8 · PREP 25 MINS

1 small cauliflower head

15g (½oz) chopped flat-leaf parsley

30g (1oz) chopped curly parsley

140g (5oz) diced cucumber

175g (6oz) diced tomato

1 small bunch spring onions, finely sliced

125g (4½oz) cooked brown lentils

15g (½oz) chopped mint leaves

zest and juice of 2 lemons

2 tbsp olive oil

salt and freshly ground black pepper

1 Remove the outer leaves from the cauliflower head and break it into florets. Place it in a food processor and pulse 6–7 times, until the cauliflower resembles rice or bulgur wheat.

2 In a large mixing bowl, combine the cauliflower, flat-leaf parsley, curly parsley, cucumber, tomato, spring onion, lentils, and mint. Add the lemon zest and juice and the olive oil and toss to combine. Season with salt and pepper to taste. Transfer to a serving dish and serve immediately.

Nutrition per serving

Calories	83
Total Fat	4g
Saturated Fat	0.5g
Cholesterol	0mg
Sodium	310mg
Total Carbohydrate	11g
Dietary Fibre	3g
Sugars	2g
Protein	4g

● **Make it with meat**

Top each serving with 85g (3oz) of sliced, grilled steak.

MUNG BEAN GADO GADO

Gado Gado is an Indonesian chopped salad whose name means *mix mix*. It's always served with spicy peanut dressing, and is accompanied here by crisp vegetables and pulses.

SERVES 4 · PREP 45 MINS

125g (4½oz) smooth peanut butter

1 tsp garlic powder

1½ tsp ground ginger

1 tsp crushed dried chillies

1½ tsp soy sauce

juice of 2 limes

1 tsp rice wine vinegar

180ml (6fl oz) water

1 small beetroot, peeled

150g (5½oz) shredded Savoy cabbage

85g (3oz) cooked mung beans

85g (3oz) cherry tomatoes, halved

30g (1oz) sprouted mung beans (beansprouts)

75g (2½oz) green beans, chopped, blanched and drained

2 hard-boiled eggs, quartered

1 To make the spicy peanut dressing, in a small bowl whisk together the peanut butter, garlic powder, ginger, crushed dried chillies, soy sauce, lime juice, and vinegar. Stir in the water until thoroughly mixed. Set aside.

2 Adjust a spiralizer to the thinnest blade and spiralize the beetroot.

3 On a large serving plate, spread the cabbage in an even layer. On top of the cabbage, arrange in separate piles the cooked mung beans, cherry tomatoes, sprouted mung beans, spiralized beetroot, green beans, and hard-boiled eggs. Serve immediately with the dressing on the side.

● **Make it vegan**

Replace the eggs with 225g (8oz) diced and seared tempeh or tofu.

● **Make it with meat**

Add to the serving plate a pile of 170g (6oz) thinly sliced, pan-seared steak.

Nutrition per serving

Calories	360
Total Fat	24g
Saturated Fat	0g
Cholesterol	255mg
Sodium	390mg
Total Carbohydrate	21g
Dietary Fibre	21g
Sugars	8g
Protein	21g

Pulse exchange

Use an equal amount of **chickpeas** in place of the cooked mung beans.

GREEN GODDESS MASON JAR SALAD

Mason jar salads are an instantly portable way to prepare healthy lunches in advance. Layering the dressing at the bottom keeps the vegetables crisp until lunchtime.

MAKES 2 · PREP 30 MINS

15g (½oz) basil leaves

3 tbsp tarragon leaves

2 tbsp finely chopped chives

60g (2oz) mayonnaise

100g (3½oz) plain Greek-style yogurt

zest and juice of 1 lemon

salt and freshly ground black pepper

85g (3oz) chopped kale

1 medium courgette

30g (1oz) sprouted mung beans (beansprouts)

60g (2oz) sliced radishes

1 To make the dressing, in a blender combine the basil, tarragon, chives, mayonnaise, yogurt, and lemon zest and juice. Blend until smooth. Season with salt and pepper to taste, and pulse once more to combine. (This makes more dressing than needed – store the remainder in an airtight container in the fridge for up to 3 days.)

2 Cut both ends off the courgette. Adjust a spiralizer to the thickest blade and spiralize the courgette. With kitchen scissors, roughly cut into bite-sized sections.

3 To assemble, place 2 tablespoons of dressing into each of 2 wide-mouthed, 475ml (16oz) jars with lids. Then layer each with equal amounts of the kale, radishes, and sprouted mung beans. Top each with half of the spiralized courgette. Secure the lids. Serve immediately or store in the fridge for up to 2 days.

● Make it with meat

Layer 30g (1oz) cooked, chopped chicken or sliced turkey in each jar, on top of the courgette.

Nutrition per jar

Calories	270
Total Fat	22g
Saturated Fat	3.5g
Cholesterol	15mg
Sodium	230mg
Total Carbohydrate	12g
Dietary Fibre	3g
Sugars	5g
Protein	10g

Pulse exchange

Use an equal amount of cooked **chickpeas** instead of the sprouted mung beans.

VEGGIE NOODLE & LENTIL SALAD

Spiralized courgette and carrot take the place of soba noodles in this light, refreshing salad.

SERVES 6 · PREP 10 MINS · COOK 20 MINS

juice of 2 large limes

2 tbsp soy sauce

1½ tsp fresh grated ginger

1¼ tbsp sesame oil

salt and freshly ground black pepper·

2 large courgettes

1 large carrot

75g (2½ oz) cooked and cooled beluga lentils

3 spring onions, chopped

15g (½ oz) chopped coriander leaves

2 tbsp toasted sesame seeds

1 To make the dressing, in a small bowl whisk together the lime juice, soy sauce, grated ginger, and sesame oil. Season with salt and pepper to taste. Set aside.

2 Cut both ends off the courgettes. Adjust a spiralizer to the medium blade and spiralize the courgettes. Add to a large mixing bowl. Spiralize the carrot and add to the mixing bowl. With kitchen scissors, trim the vegetables into shorter lengths.

3 Incorporate the beluga lentils and spring onions. Drizzle the dressing over the salad and toss to combine. Garnish with the coriander and toasted sesame seeds. Serve immediately.

Nutrition per serving

Calories	100
Total Fat	4g
Saturated Fat	0.5g
Cholesterol	0mg
Sodium	560mg
Total Carbohydrate	13g
Dietary Fibre	4g
Sugars	3g
Protein	5g

● **Make it vegan**

Instead of soy sauce, use an equal amount of liquid aminos.

RADICCHIO & BEAN SALAD

Radicchio's mild bitterness blends with creamy haricot beans in this chopped salad.

SERVES 6 · PREP 25 MINS

10g (¼oz) parsley leaves

5g (⅛oz) basil leaves

1 large garlic clove

1 tsp Dijon mustard

2 tbsp white balsamic vinegar

1 tsp honey

80ml (3fl oz) olive oil

salt and freshly ground black pepper

450g (1lb) cooked haricot beans

1 small head radicchio

(115g) 4oz feta cheese, crumbled

1 Reserve 2 tablespoons of parsley for the garnish. To make the dressing, in a food processor, combine the remaining parsley, basil, garlic, mustard, vinegar, and honey. With the food processor running, drizzle in the oil and process until smooth. Season with salt and pepper to taste.

2 In a large mixing bowl, combine the haricot beans and dressing and stir to thoroughly coat.

3 Discard the core and outer leaves of the radicchio. Rinse and dry the leaves. Roughly chop, add to the mixing bowl, and toss to combine.

4 Transfer to a serving dish and garnish with the feta and reserved parsley. Serve immediately.

Nutrition per serving

Calories	250
Total Fat	15g
Saturated Fat	4.5g
Cholesterol	20mg
Sodium	200mg
Total Carbohydrate	20g
Dietary Fibre	7g
Sugars	3g
Protein	8g

● **Make it with meat**

Crisp 100g (4oz) Parma ham and crumble over the top with the feta.

LARB CABBAGE CUPS
WITH SPROUTS & TOFU

Crisp cabbage cups are the perfect vessel for the bold, umami-packed flavours of Thai larb. Sprouted lentils and mung beans add a unique twist to this vegetarian version.

MAKES 8 · PREP 30 MINS · COOK 20 MINS

● **Make it with meat**

For a more traditional, meat-based larb, replace the tofu with 350g (12oz) cooked minced chicken or duck.

juice of 3 large limes

2 tbsp rice wine vinegar

2 garlic cloves, finely chopped

1 tsp grated fresh ginger

2 tbsp soy sauce

2 Thai red chillies, deseeded and finely chopped

2½ tbsp sesame oil

350g (12oz) extra firm block tofu, drained

30g (1oz) sprouted brown lentils

75g (2½oz) sprouted mung beans (beansprouts)

10g (¼oz) chopped mint leaves

10g (¼oz) chopped coriander leaves

8 small leaves Savoy cabbage or iceberg lettuce

75g (2½oz) roasted, unsalted peanuts, chopped

1 To make the dressing, in a large mixing bowl whisk together the lime juice, vinegar, garlic, ginger, soy sauce, and chillies. Set aside.

2 Blot the tofu with kitchen paper to absorb the moisture, then roughly chop. In a medium frying pan, warm the sesame oil over a medium heat. Add the tofu. With a spatula or wooden spoon, crumble it up into small pieces. Cook for 10–12 minutes until dry and lightly browned.

3 In the large mixing bowl, combine the tofu and dressing. Add the sprouted lentils, sprouted mung beans, mint, and coriander. Stir to combine. Divide the tofu mixture equally among the cabbage leaves. Garnish with a sprinkle of chopped peanuts. Serve immediately.

Nutrition per cabbage cup

Calories	180
Total Fat	11g
Saturated Fat	1.5g
Cholesterol	0mg
Sodium	280mg
Total Carbohydrate	12g
Dietary Fibre	5g
Sugars	4g
Protein	9g

Pulse exchange

Use 250g (9oz) cooked **mung beans** instead of sprouted mung beans.

ROASTED TOMATOES & WHITE BEANS
WITH BASIL VINAIGRETTE

Lush and flavourful roasted tomatoes are combined here with a fresh and healthy green vinaigrette for a tasty side dish.

SERVES 4 · PREP 15 MINS · COOK 30 MINS

4 plum tomatoes

3 tbsp olive oil

2 garlic cloves, finely chopped

20g (¾oz) basil leaves

60ml (2fl oz) white wine or Champagne vinegar

salt and freshly ground black pepper

350g (12oz) cooked cannellini or flageolet beans

1 Preheat the oven to 200°C (400°F). Cut the tomatoes in half lengthways and toss with the garlic and 1 tablespoon of oil. Arrange on a baking tray and roast for 30 minutes. Let cool to room temperature.

2 Meanwhile, to make the basil vinaigrette, in a blender or food processor add the basil and vinegar. With the processor running on low, drizzle in the remaining 2 tablespoons of oil until emulsified. Season with salt and pepper to taste.

3 In a mixing bowl, toss the cannellini beans with 2 tablespoons of dressing and spread on a serving plate. Arrange the roasted tomatoes on top. Season with salt and pepper. Garnish with any remaining dressing and basil leaves. Serve immediately.

Nutrition per serving

Calories	214
Total Fat	10g
Saturated Fat	1.5g
Cholesterol	0mg
Sodium	591mg
Total Carbohydrate	22g
Dietary Fibre	7g
Sugars	1.7g
Protein	8.5g

● **Make it with meat**

Add 100g (4oz) grilled prawns on top of the beans.

TOMATO LENTIL SALAD
WITH GRILLED HALLOUMI

The contrasting textures of al dente lentils and soft, tangy halloumi cheese make this salad extra special.

SERVES 4 · PREP 20 MINS · COOK 15 MINS

1 small shallot, chopped

1 large garlic clove, finely chopped

juice and zest of 1 lemon

1 tsp chopped thyme

1 tsp chopped oregano

2 tbsp olive oil

900g (2lb) cooked green or Puy lentils

350g (12oz) cherry or baby plum tomatoes, halved

salt and freshly ground black pepper

225g (8oz) halloumi cheese

1 In a medium mixing bowl, whisk together the shallot, garlic, lemon juice and zest, thyme, oregano, and oil. Add the lentils and tomatoes. Leave to marinate while you grill the halloumi.

2 Heat a large non-stick frying pan or ridged cast-iron grill pan over a medium heat. Cut the halloumi into 8 equal slices and place in the pan. Cook for 2–3 minutes on each side, until browned and soft.

3 Arrange the lentil-tomato mixture on a serving plate and top with the slices of warm halloumi. Serve immediately.

● **Make it with meat**

Add 60g (2oz) cooked, sliced chorizo to the lentil salad.

Nutrition per serving

Calories	451
Total Fat	22g
Saturated Fat	11g
Cholesterol	38mg
Sodium	843mg
Total Carbohydrate	42g
Dietary Fibre	12g
Sugars	4g
Protein	26g

Pulse exchange

If you don't have green or Puy lentils, use an equal amount of **brown lentils**.

MOTH BEANS & GRILLED ROMAINE
WITH RED PEPPER VINAIGRETTE

Grilled lettuce may seem unusual, but it adds a deliciously subtle smoky flavour and a layer of depth to green salads.

SERVES 6 · PREP 20 MINS · COOK 20 MINS

100g (3½oz) roasted red peppers from a jar, drained

1 large garlic clove

1 tbsp red wine vinegar

½ tsp chopped oregano

1 tsp chopped basil leaves

3 tbsp olive oil

salt and freshly ground black pepper

3 romaine lettuce hearts

175g (6oz) cooked moth beans, or black lentils

115g (4oz) soft goat's cheese

1 In a food processor, combine the red peppers, garlic, vinegar, oregano, and basil. With the processor running, drizzle in 2 tablespoons of oil. Season with salt and pepper to taste.

2 Carefully cut each romaine heart in half lengthways, leaving as much of the core intact as possible. Drizzle with the remaining 1 tablespoon of oil. On a preheated ridged cast-iron grill pan, cook the romaine for 1–3 minutes on each side, until slightly wilted and charred but not cooked through.

3 Arrange the lettuce on a large serving plate. Scatter the mung beans evenly across the top. Crumble the goat's cheese over, and top with dressing to taste. Garnish with black pepper and serve immediately.

● **Make it vegan**

Omit the goat's cheese and substitute a nut-based vegan cheese alternative.

● **Make it with meat**

Top with 125g (4½ oz) cooked, chopped chicken or turkey before adding the cheese.

Nutrition per serving

Calories	200
Total Fat	13g
Saturated Fat	5g
Cholesterol	15mg
Sodium	390mg
Total Carbohydrate	14g
Dietary Fibre	7g
Sugars	4g
Protein	9g

Why not try... For an extra briny kick, garnish the salad with 3–4 tablespoons of capers.

SWEET POTATO & BELUGA LENTIL SALAD
DRESSED WITH HONEY & LEMON

The firm nuttiness of the lentils and the soft, caramelized sweet potato makes a wonderful combination of flavours and textures.

SERVES 2 · PREP 25 MINS, PLUS COOLING · COOK 45 MINS

1 large sweet potato, peeled and diced

⅛ tsp smoked paprika

2 tbsp olive oil

salt and freshly ground black pepper

750ml (1¼ pints) water

325g (11oz) uncooked beluga lentils

2 spring onions, trimmed and finely sliced

1 large celery stick, diced, leafy parts reserved for garnish

30g (1oz) feta cheese, crumbled

1 tbsp honey or agave nectar

juice of 1 lemon

1 Preheat the oven to 180°C (350°F). On a baking tray, toss the sweet potato and paprika in 1 tablespoon of oil. Season with salt and pepper. Roast until tender and slightly caramelized, about 25 minutes, stirring once halfway. Let cool to room temperature.

2 Meanwhile, in a medium saucepan, bring the water to the boil. Add the lentils and return to the boil for 2–3 minutes. Reduce to a simmer and cook, covered, for 25–30 minutes, until tender but not soft. Drain in a fine colander and let cool to room temperature.

3 To assemble, in a large mixing bowl combine the lentils, sweet potatoes, onion, celery, and feta. Mix well. Drizzle in the honey, lemon juice, and remaining 1 tablespoon of oil. Toss to combine. Season with salt and pepper to taste. Garnish with the reserved celery leaves. Serve at room temperature.

Make it vegan

Use a nut-based vegan cheese alternative rather than feta.

Make it with meat

Add 4 crumbled rashers of crispy bacon to the lentil-feta mixture in step 3.

Nutrition per serving

Calories	480
Total Fat	19g
Saturated Fat	5g
Cholesterol	15mg
Sodium	1380mg
Total Carbohydrate	63g
Dietary Fibre	11g
Sugars	16g
Protein	17g

Pulse exchange

Substitute an equal amount uncooked **brown** or **green lentils** for the beluga lentils.

CHICKPEA & CHERRY SALAD

This salad combines the flavours of summer in a single bowl. The tart sweetness of the cherries contrasts with the nuttiness of the chickpeas to create an unusual side dish.

SERVES 4 · PREP 15 MINS

3 tbsp apple cider vinegar

1 tbsp olive oil

1 tsp honey

350g (12oz) cooked chickpeas

175g (6oz) dark, sweet cherries, pitted

2 tbsp chopped basil leaves

45g (1½oz) ricotta salata cheese, crumbled

salt and freshly ground black pepper

1 To make the dressing, in a small bowl whisk together the vinegar, oil, and honey. Set aside.

2 In a large salad bowl, add the chickpeas. Cut the cherries in half and combine with the chickpeas. Add the basil and mix thoroughly. Drizzle the dressing over and toss to evenly coat.

3 Top with the crumbled ricotta salata. Season with salt and pepper to taste and serve immediately.

Nutrition per serving

Calories	220
Total Fat	8g
Saturated Fat	2.5g
Cholesterol	10mg
Sodium	380mg
Total Carbohydrate	30g
Dietary Fibre	8g
Sugars	10g
Protein	9g

● Make it vegan

Omit the ricotta salata and use 60g (2oz) capers to add a salty tang.

POTATO SALAD
WITH DIJON & LENTILS

Lentils elevate this potato salad with extra texture and lots of nutritious protein.

SERVES 6 · PREP 10 MINS · COOK 10 MINS

675g (1½lb) small potatoes, quartered

50g (1¾oz) plain Greek-style yogurt

2 tbsp mayonnaise

1½ tsp Dijon mustard

1½ tsp wholegrain mustard

1 tsp red wine vinegar

150g (5½oz) cooked beluga lentils

3 spring onions, chopped

1 tbsp chopped chervil or parsley

salt and freshly ground black pepper

1 Bring a large saucepan of water to the boil. Add the potatoes and cook for 10 minutes, or until tender to the point of a knife. Drain thoroughly.

2 Meanwhile, in a large mixing bowl, whisk together the yogurt, mayonnaise, Dijon mustard, wholegrain mustard, and red wine vinegar. Fold in the cooked potatoes and the beluga lentils.

3 Add the spring onions and chervil and stir to combine thoroughly. Season with salt and pepper to taste. Serve immediately or store in an airtight container for up to 2 days.

Nutrition per serving

Calories	250
Total Fat	6g
Saturated Fat	0.5g
Cholesterol	<5g
Sodium	230g
Total Carbohydrate	42g
Dietary Fibre	8g
Sugars	3g
Protein	11g

● **Make it with meat**

For extra punch, stir in 140g (5oz) of crispy bacon or Parma ham, diced.

BLACK-EYED BEAN FATTOUSH

Toasted bread, crisp vegetables, and lemony herbs add brightness to this hearty salad.

SERVES 8 · PREP 25 MINS · COOK 8 MINS

2 wholewheat pittas, torn into 3cm (1in) pieces

1 garlic clove, finely chopped

1 tsp sumac

4 tbsp olive oil

2 tbsp lemon juice

salt and pepper

1 large cucumber, peeled, deseeded, and diced

85g (3oz) baby plum tomatoes, halved

1 yellow pepper, deseeded and diced

175g (6oz) cooked black-eyed beans

5g (⅛oz) chopped flat-leaf parsley

10g (¼oz) chopped mint leaves

1 Preheat the oven to 190°C (375°F). On a baking sheet, arrange the pitta in a single layer. Toast for 8 minutes, or until crisp and light golden brown. Remove from the oven and leave to cool.

2 To make the dressing, in a small bowl whisk together the garlic, sumac, oil, and lemon juice. Season with salt and pepper to taste. Set aside.

3 In a large mixing bowl, combine the cucumber, tomato, yellow pepper, and black-eyed beans, and drizzle in the dressing. Add the parsley and mint and toss to combine. Add the toasted pitta and toss again. Season with salt and pepper to taste. Serve immediately.

Nutrition per serving

Calories	170
Total Fat	10g
Saturated Fat	1.5g
Cholesterol	0mg
Sodium	480mg
Total Carbohydrate	20g
Dietary Fibre	5g
Sugars	2g
Protein	5g

● **Make it with meat**

Add 450g (1lb) grilled chicken or steak, chopped, along with the pitta in step 3.

CHICKPEA & KALE CAESAR SALAD

Chickpeas make two appearances in this Caesar salad. They're the creamy emulsifier in the garlicky dressing, and they're the crispy and nutritious alternative to croutons.

SERVES 6 · PREP 20 MINS · COOK 5 MINS

1 bunch of kale

250g (9oz) cooked chickpeas

1 tbsp mayonnaise or plain Greek-style yogurt

2 tsp Dijon mustard

2 garlic cloves

juice of 2 lemons

240ml (8fl oz) olive oil

20g (¾oz) grated Parmesan cheese (optional)

1 On clean kitchen paper, arrange 175g (6oz) cooked chickpeas in a single layer. Leave to air dry.

2 Remove and discard the tough ribs and stems from the kale and chop the leaves into bite-sized pieces. Rinse to remove any grit and drain.

3 Meanwhile, to make the dressing, in a blender combine the remaining 75g (3oz) chickpeas, mayonnaise, Dijon mustard, garlic, and lemon juice. With the blender running, drizzle in 120ml (4fl oz) oil and blend until smooth. Set aside.

4 In a medium frying pan, heat the remaining 120ml (4fl oz) oil over a medium-high heat. Once shimmering, carefully add the dried chickpeas and fry for 3–4 minutes until crisp and golden brown. Remove and place on a plate lined with kitchen paper to absorb excess oil.

5 In a large mixing bowl, toss together the kale and dressing, using your hands to massage and thoroughly coat the kale. Transfer to serving plates and top with the fried chickpeas. If using, sprinkle over the grated Parmesan. Serve immediately.

Nutrition per serving

Calories	270
Total Fat	20g
Saturated Fat	3.5g
Cholesterol	<5mg
Sodium	125mg
Total Carbohydrate	17g
Dietary Fibre	4g
Sugars	2g
Protein	7g

● Make it vegan

Replace the mayonnaise with plain soya yogurt and replace the Parmesan with nutritional yeast.

● Make it with meat

For extra protein, top the salad with grilled, sliced chicken breast.

Why not try... For a splash of colour, add 85g (3oz) halved cherry or baby plum tomatoes.

BUTTER BEAN PANZANELLA

Panzanella is a Tuscan bread salad popular in the warmer months. It's a great use for day-old bread and wonderful for parties and picnics, as it can be served at room temperature.

SERVES 6 · PREP 25 MINS · COOK 15 MINS

1 small loaf sourdough bread

60ml (2fl oz) red wine vinegar

1 tbsp Dijon mustard

120ml (4fl oz) olive oil

2 garlic cloves, finely chopped

1 tsp chopped oregano

1 tsp chopped basil leaves

175g (6oz) cherry tomatoes, halved

225g (8oz) cooked butter beans

1 cucumber, diced

150g (5½oz) fresh sweetcorn kernels

salt and freshly ground black pepper

1 Preheat the oven to 170°C (325°F). Cut the bread into 1cm (½in) cubes. On a baking sheet, arrange the bread cubes in a single layer and bake for 15 minutes, or until toasted and light golden brown.

2 Meanwhile, to make the dressing, in a small bowl whisk together the vinegar and Dijon mustard. While whisking, drizzle in the oil and thoroughly combine. Stir in the garlic, oregano, and basil. Set aside.

3 To assemble, in a large salad bowl, add the tomatoes, butter beans, cucumber, and sweetcorn. Fold in the toasted bread, then drizzle the dressing over. Toss to coat. Season with salt and pepper to taste. Serve immediately.

Nutrition per serving

Calories	430
Total Fat	12g
Saturated Fat	2g
Cholesterol	0mg
Sodium	380mg
Total Carbohydrate	69g
Dietary Fiber	9g
Sugars	5g
Protein	14g

● **Make it with meat**

Add 115g (4oz) cooked prawns when you assemble the salad.

BURGERS, TACOS & SANDWICHES

MUNG BEAN BURGERS
WITH RED CURRY AIOLI

Mung beans provide this textured veggie burger with great bite and a lovely green colour.

MAKES 6 · PREP 25 MINS · COOK 25 MINS

● **Make it vegan**

Mix 2 tablespoons flax seeds with 6 tablespoons water to replace each egg. Replace the Greek yogurt with coconut yogurt.

1 shallot, finely chopped

1 garlic cloves, finely chopped

350g (12oz) cooked mung beans

¼ tsp ground coriander

pinch of crushed dried chillies

2 tbsp chopped coriander leaves

1 tbsp chopped mint leaves

2 large eggs, beaten

20g (¾oz) panko breadcrumbs

salt and freshly ground black pepper

100g (3½oz) plain Greek-style yogurt

½ tbsp red curry paste

6 hamburger buns or small pittas

1 Preheat the oven to 190°C (375°F). Line a baking sheet with baking parchment or spray with cooking spray. In a large mixing bowl, combine the shallot, garlic, mung beans, ground coriander, chillies, coriander leaves, and mint. With a pastry cutter or the back of a fork, lightly mash the mixture, allowing about half the mung beans to remain intact.

2 Add the eggs and stir to mix thoroughly. Gently fold in the breadcrumbs and season with salt and pepper.

3 Divide the mung bean mixture into 6 equal portions. Use a measuring cup to place a rounded portion onto the baking sheet and lightly flatten it to make a burger. Repeat to make 6 in total. Bake for 10 minutes on each side, carefully turning in between.

4 Meanwhile, to make the red curry aioli, in a small mixing bowl whisk together the yogurt and red curry paste. Season with salt and pepper to taste.

5 To assemble, spread the curry aioli on the bottom half of the bun or inside of the pitta and add the burger. Repeat for the remaining burgers and serve immediately.

Nutrition per burger

Calories	360
Total Fat	17g
Saturated Fat	3g
Cholesterol	70mg
Sodium	400mg
Total Carbohydrate	37g
Dietary Fibre	5g
Sugars	5g
Protein	13g

Why not try...

For a double dose of legumes and texture, top your burger with alfalfa sprouts.

RED LENTIL & SWEET POTATO CROQUETTES

These croquettes are a lovely balance of sweet and savoury. They make an excellent side dish, or a main course when served with a crisp green salad.

MAKES 12 · PREP 10 MINS · COOK 1 HR 30 MINS

● **Make it vegan**

Mix 2 tablespoons flax seeds with 6 tablespoons water to replace each egg.

175g (6oz) uncooked red lentils

1 large sweet potato, diced

2 large eggs, separately beaten

½ tsp cinnamon

¼ tsp paprika

½ tsp ground cayenne pepper

zest of 1 orange

115g (4oz) panko breadcrumbs

salt and freshly ground black pepper

240ml (8fl oz) vegetable oil

1 In a medium saucepan, cover the lentils with about 5cm (2in) cold water. Cover and bring to the boil, then reduce to a simmer and cook for 20 minutes, or until completely tender. Let sit in a colander for at least 30 minutes, or until completely drained.

2 Meanwhile, bring a large saucepan of water to the boil. Add the sweet potatoes and cook, covered, for 20 minutes, or until tender to the point of a knife. Let sit for 30 minutes, or until completely drained.

3 In a food processor, purée the sweet potatoes until smooth. Transfer to a large mixing bowl and incorporate the red lentils, 1 egg, the cinnamon, paprika, cayenne, orange zest, and one-third of the breadcrumbs. Season with salt and pepper. Refrigerate for 15 minutes, or until cool.

4 In a shallow dish, add the remaining egg. In another shallow dish, add the remaining breadcrumbs. With your hands, form the lentil mixture into 5cm (2-in) cylindrical croquettes. Dredge in the egg then gently roll in the breadcrumbs until coated.

5 In a deep 30cm (12in) cast-iron frying pan, heat the oil over a medium heat until shimmering. Working in batches, place the croquettes in the oil, turning every 1–2 minutes until brown on all sides. Remove and place on a plate lined with kitchen paper. Serve immediately.

Nutrition per croquette

Calories	150
Total Fat	7g
Saturated Fat	5g
Cholesterol	30mg
Sodium	230mg
Total Carbohydrate	17g
Dietary Fibre	3g
Sugars	1g
Protein	6g

Pulse exchange

Use an equal amount of **yellow lentils** instead of the red lentils.

INDIAN POTATO & CHICKPEA PATTIES

The golden hue and warm Indian spices in these patties are reminiscent of dosa, the traditional South Indian potato-stuffed pancake. Serve these with chutney and raita.

MAKES 14 · PREP 25 MINS · COOK 1 HR

750g (1lb 10oz) peeled and diced potatoes, about 7–8 potatoes

250g (9oz) cooked chickpeas

3 tbsp ghee

1 small red onion, finely diced

1 garlic clove, finely chopped

1½ tsp garam masala

1 tsp ground ginger

¾ tsp ground coriander

75g (2½oz) cooked green peas

45g (1½oz) panko breadcrumbs

salt and freshly ground black pepper

10g (¼oz) chopped coriander leaves, for garnish

1 Bring a large stock pot full of water to the boil. Add the potatoes and cook for 20 minutes, or until tender to the point of a knife. Drain and leave to dry in a colander for 15 minutes.

2 In a large mixing bowl, with a potato masher roughly mash the chickpeas. Add the potatoes and mash again to combine.

3 In a medium non-stick frying pan, heat 1 tablespoon ghee over a medium-low heat. Add the onion and cook for 2–3 minutes until soft. Add the garlic and cook for an additional minute. Stir in the garam masala, ginger, and ground coriander. Cook for an additional minute to warm the spices.

4 In the mixing bowl, combine the onion mixture with the potato-chickpea mixture. Add the remaining 2 tablespoons ghee and stir to combine. Stir in the green peas and breadcrumbs. Mix thoroughly then season with salt and pepper to taste.

5 Using your hands, form into patties and place in a non-stick frying pan over a medium-low heat for 4–5 minutes on each side, until warmed through and lightly golden brown, adjusting the heat as necessary to prevent burning. Work in batches to form and cook the mixture, making about 14 patties in total. Garnish with chopped coriander and serve immediately.

● **Make it vegan**

Instead of ghee, use rapeseed or any vegetable oil.

Nutrition per patty

Calories	100
Total Fat	4g
Saturated Fat	2g
Cholesterol	5g
Sodium	15g
Total Carbohydrate	13g
Dietary Fibre	3g
Sugars	2g
Protein	3g

Why not try...
For heat, cook one small green chilli, deseeded and finely chopped, with the garlic and onion.

BLACK-EYED BEAN SLIDERS
WITH PICO DE GALLO

The pico de gallo adds a wonderful texture and moisture to these creamy black-eyed bean burgers.

MAKES 8 · PREP 30 MINS · COOK 20 MINS

1 tbsp plus 1 tsp olive oil

2 small onions, diced

1 garlic clove, finely chopped

2 small jalapeños, deseeded and diced, about 3 tbsp in total

½ tsp chipotle chilli powder

2½ tsp ground cumin

450g (1lb) cooked black-eyed beans

2 large eggs, beaten

20g (¾oz) panko breadcrumbs

1 large tomato, deseeded and diced

10g (¼oz) chopped coriander leaves

juice of 1 large lime

8 slider-sized burger buns

1 Preheat the oven to 150°C (300°F). In a large non-stick frying pan, heat the oil over a medium-low heat until shimmering. Add one of the onions and cook for 2 minutes, or until soft. Add the garlic and half the jalapeño. Cook for 2 minutes. Transfer to a large mixing bowl and set aside. Set aside the frying pan, leaving any residual oil in the pan.

2 Add the chipotle chilli powder, cumin, black-eyed beans, eggs, and breadcrumbs to the vegetable mixture. With a potato masher, mix to combine and break up the beans slightly.

3 Return the frying pan to the stove and heat over a medium heat. Divide the mixture into 8 equal portions and use your hands to form into patties. In batches, cook for 3–4 minutes on each side, pressing lightly with a spatula to sear. Transfer the patties to a baking sheet. Repeat to use all the mixture, adding ½ teaspoon oil to the frying pan between batches. Transfer the baking sheet to the oven and bake for 8–10 minutes until cooked through.

4 Meanwhile, to make the pico de gallo, in a small bowl combine the tomato, the remaining diced onion, remaining jalapeño, chopped coriander, and lime juice. To assemble, place each burger on a slider bun and top with 1 tablespoon of pico de gallo. Serve immediately.

Nutrition per slider

Calories	230
Total Fat	6g
Saturated Fat	1g
Cholesterol	75mg
Sodium	290mg
Total Carbohydrate	34g
Dietary Fibre	5g
Sugars	4g
Protein	9g

Why not try...
Give these sliders more crunch by topping with shredded green or red cabbage.

PIGEON PEA PATTIES
WITH GUAVA SAUCE

These patties have all the spice found in Jamaican jerk seasoning balanced with the sweet heat of a guava glaze.

MAKES 10 · PREP 30 MINS · COOK 45 MINS

● **Make it vegan**

Instead of eggs, use half a ripe avocado.

175g (6oz) guava jelly

2 tbsp red wine vinegar

¼ tsp crushed dried chillies

2 tbsp vegetable oil or rapeseed oil

1 small red onion, finely diced

1 Serrano chilli, deseeded and finely chopped

1 garlic clove, finely chopped

½ tsp cinnamon

1 tsp ground cumin

¾ tsp ground nutmeg

1¼ tsp allspice

¼ tsp ground cayenne pepper

450g (1lb) cooked pigeon peas, or black-eyed beans

20g (¾oz) panko breadcrumbs

2 large eggs, beaten

3 tbsp chopped coriander, leaves, to garnish

1 To make the guava sauce, in a small saucepan combine the guava jelly, red wine vinegar, and crushed dried chillies. Simmer over a low heat for 8–10 minutes, until melted and syrupy. Remove from the heat and keep warm on the stove.

2 Meanwhile, in a medium frying pan, heat 1 tablespoon of oil over a medium-low heat. Add the onion and cook for 2–3 minutes until soft. Then add the Serrano chilli and garlic and cook for an additional 1–2 minutes. Add the cinnamon, cumin, nutmeg, allspice, cayenne, and 375g (13oz) pigeon peas (or black-eyed beans). Stir to combine.

3 Transfer the pigeon pea mixture to a food processor. Pulse until slightly puréed. Then transfer to a large mixing bowl and add the breadcrumbs, eggs, and remaining 75g (3oz) whole pigeon peas (or black-eyed beans). Fold together to combine.

4 Wipe out the frying pan and return to the stove. Heat the remaining 1 tablespoon of oil over a medium-low heat. Divide the pigeon pea mixture into 10 round portions and place one in the frying pan, slightly flattening it with a spatula. Cook for 3–4 minutes on each side until golden brown.

5 Repeat with the remaining mixture, adding oil to the frying pan as necessary. Serve immediately with guava sauce.

Nutrition per patty

Calories	180
Total Fat	4g
Saturated Fat	0.5g
Cholesterol	35g
Sodium	20g
Total Carbohydrate	26g
Dietary Fibre	4g
Sugars	9g
Protein	5g

BLACK-EYED BEAN & COLLARD GREEN TACOS

Black-eyed beans and greens are a classic pairing. Here, with some creamy goat's cheese and a splash of hot sauce, they make a unique taco filling.

MAKES 12 · PREP 20 MINS · COOK 40 MINS

1 tbsp olive oil

1 small onion, finely diced

1 garlic clove, finely chopped

250g (9oz) collard greens (or kale), rinsed and roughly chopped

475ml (16fl oz) vegetable stock

½ tsp white wine vinegar

⅛ tsp ground cayenne pepper

375g (13oz) cooked black-eyed beans

salt and freshly ground black pepper

12 corn tortillas

175g (6oz) goat's cheese

hot sauce (optional)

1 In a medium flameproof casserole or heavy-based saucepan, heat the oil over a medium-low heat until shimmering. Add the onion and cook for 2–3 minutes until soft. Add the garlic and cook for another minute.

2 Stir in the greens. Add the stock, vinegar, and cayenne. Bring to the boil then reduce to a simmer and cook, covered, for 20 minutes, or until the greens are tender. Add the black-eyed beans and cook for an additional 10 minutes, or until the beans are warmed through and most of the liquid has evaporated. Season with salt and pepper to taste.

3 Warm the tortillas in a frying pan. To assemble, place one tortilla on a flat, clean work surface. Using a slotted spoon to drain away some of the liquid, place a portion of the beans and greens mixture onto the tortilla. Sprinkle with goat's cheese and a few dashes of hot sauce, if using. Roll the taco, then repeat with remaining ingredients to make 12 tacos in total. Serve immediately.

Make it vegan

Omit the goat's cheese or use a non-dairy cheese alternative.

Make it with meat

Add 75g (2½oz) cooked smoked turkey or pork, chopped, along with the greens in step 2.

Nutrition per taco

Calories	120
Total Fat	4.5g
Saturated Fat	2g
Cholesterol	5mg
Sodium	110mg
Total Carbohydrate	16g
Dietary Fibre	4g
Sugars	1g
Protein	6g

Why not try...
Add a spoonful of your favourite salsa to each taco after the goat's cheese and hot sauce.

SPIRALIZED BEETROOT & KIDNEY BEAN PATTIES

The hot pink colour and texture from the beetroot is truly special. Serve these as you would your favourite veggie burger or alongside grilled chicken or pork.

MAKES 8 · PREP 15 MINS · COOK 30 MINS

2 beetroots, peeled

350g (12oz) cooked kidney beans

1 tbsp chopped spring onion

1 tbsp chopped coriander leaves

pinch of crushed dried chillies

45g (1½oz) panko breadcrumbs

2 large eggs, beaten

salt and freshly ground black pepper

1 Preheat the oven to 170°C (325°F). Line a baking sheet with baking parchment.

2 Adjust a spiralizer to the medium blade and spiralize the beetroots. With kitchen scissors, cut the strands into about 3cm (1in) pieces.

3 In a large mixing bowl, gently mash the kidney beans with a fork or pastry cutter, so some beans remain intact. Fold in the spiralized beetroot, spring onion, coriander, crushed dried chillies, breadcrumbs, and eggs. Season with salt and pepper.

4 Heat a large non-stick frying pan over a medium heat. Form the mixture into 8 equal patties. Place the patties in the frying pan and cook for 3–4 minutes on each side until brown and holding together. Arrange on the baking sheet.

5 Bake the patties for 8–10 minutes until cooked through. Serve immediately.

Make it vegan

Replace the eggs with an extra 85g (3oz) cooked kidney beans and 2 tablespoons water, puréed in a food processor, and add to the mixture in step 3.

Nutrition per patty

Calories	100
Total Fat	1.5g
Saturated Fat	0g
Cholesterol	45mg
Sodium	330mg
Total Carbohydrate	16g
Dietary Fibre	4g
Sugars	2g
Protein	6g

Pulse exchange

Use an equal amount of **pinto beans** instead of kidney beans.

RAINBOW LENTIL MEATBALLS
WITH ARRABIATTA SAUCE

Lentil meatballs and spicy tomato sauce are a vegetarian alternative to the comfort food classic, loaded with protein and fibre. Serve with pasta or bread and Parmesan cheese.

MAKES 18 · PREP 15 MINS · COOK 40 MINS

300g (10oz) cooked red lentils, thoroughly drained

85g (3oz) cooked brown lentils, thoroughly drained

1 large egg, lightly beaten

45g (1½oz) panko breadcrumbs

½ tsp garlic powder

1 tsp dried oregano

zest of 1 large lemon

¼ tsp ground cayenne pepper

2 tbsp olive oil

1 small onion, finely chopped

2 x 400g (14oz) cans chopped tomatoes

1 tbsp crushed dried chillies

salt and freshly ground black pepper

1 Preheat the oven to 180°C (350°F). Lightly oil a baking tray. In a large mixing bowl, combine the red lentils, brown lentils, egg, breadcrumbs, garlic powder, oregano, lemon zest, and cayenne.

2 With your hands, form approximately 1 tablespoon of the lentil mixture into a meatball and place on the baking tray. Repeat with the remaining mixture. Bake for 25 minutes, rotating the meatballs halfway through.

3 Meanwhile, to make the arrabiatta sauce, in a saucepan warm the oil over a medium-low heat. Add the onion and cook for 2 minutes, or until soft. Add the tomatoes and chillies. Simmer over a low heat for 15 minutes, or until the sauce is warmed through. Season with salt and pepper to taste.

4 Place the meatballs on serving plates, top with the sauce, and serve immediately.

Nutrition per meatball

Calories	70
Total Fat	2g
Saturated Fat	0g
Cholesterol	0mg
Sodium	115mg
Total Carbohydrate	9g
Dietary Fibre	2g
Sugars	2g
Protein	3g

● Make it with meat

Add 225g (8oz) minced beef or crumbled Italian sausage along with the onion in step 3.

YELLOW LENTIL & QUINOA CAKES

These little cakes come together quickly and make a great lunch served with a salad.

MAKES 10 · PREP 10 MINS · COOK 45 MINS

150g (5½oz) cooked yellow lentils

⅛ tsp garlic powder

3 spring onions, chopped

2 tbsp chopped basil

2 tbsp chopped oregano

4 large eggs, beaten

75g (2½oz) panko breadcrumbs

550g (1¼lb) cooked quinoa

1 tbsp olive oil

1 In a large mixing bowl, combine the yellow lentils, garlic powder, spring onions, basil, oregano, eggs, and breadcrumbs. Fold the quinoa into the lentil mixture and mix thoroughly.

2 Divide the mixture into 10 equal portions. On a damp plate, gently shape one portion into a small, flattened patty. Repeat to make 10 patties in total and let sit for 5 minutes.

3 Meanwhile, in a medium non-stick frying pan, heat the oil over a medium heat. Place the patties in the frying pan. Cook for 2–3 minutes on each side until golden and holding together. Serve immediately.

Nutrition per patty

Calories	170
Total Fat	5g
Saturated Fat	1g
Cholesterol	75mg
Sodium	45mg
Total Carbohydrate	23g
Dietary Fibre	4g
Sugars	1g
Protein	7g

● **Make it vegan**

Replace each egg with 3 tablespoons of mashed potatoes.

BEAN FLAUTAS
WITH AVOCADO CREMA

Meaty Scarlet Runner beans and cheese fill these baked Mexican treats.

MAKES 16 · PREP 20 MINS · COOK 10 MINS

240ml (8fl oz) soured cream

1 avocado, halved

juice of 1 lime

175g (6oz) cooked Scarlet Runner beans, or kidney beans

115g (4oz) mature Cheddar cheese, grated

115g (4oz) goat's cheese

45g (1½oz) chopped spring onion

85g (3oz) fresh sweetcorn kernels

15g (½oz) chopped coriander leaves

1 tbsp ground cumin

1 tsp cayenne pepper

16 small flour tortillas

1 Preheat the oven to 200°C (400°F). Set up a wire rack on a baking tray. To make the crema, in a food processor or blender, combine the soured cream, avocado flesh, and lime juice until smooth. Transfer to a small bowl and refrigerate.

2 In a large mixing bowl, lightly mash the Scarlet Runners with a potato masher. Incorporate the cheeses, spring onion, sweetcorn, coriander, cumin, and cayenne. Season with salt to taste.

3 To assemble, place 2 tablespoons of filling at one edge of a tortilla, and tightly roll, leaving the ends open. Place seam-side down on the wire rack. Repeat to make 16 flautas in total. Bake for 20 minutes, or until the edges are lightly browned. Serve immediately with the crema on the side.

Nutrition per flauta

Calories	210
Total Fat	8g
Saturated Fat	4g
Cholesterol	10mg
Sodium	440mg
Total Carbohydrate	25g
Dietary Fibre	3g
Sugars	1g
Protein	10g

● **Make it with meat**

Add 140g (5oz) cooked, chopped chicken or beef to the filling when you add the cheese. This yields at least 20 flautas.

HARISSA RED LENTIL MEATBALLS

These spicy lentil meatballs are an all-purpose vegetarian meal. Serve along with pasta, your choice of sauce, or even tucked into a pitta.

MAKES 18 · PREP 30 MINS · COOK 35 MINS

1 yellow squash, or yellow courgette

3 tbsp olive oil

1 small onion, diced

1 garlic clove, finely chopped

450g (1lb) cooked red lentils

60g (2oz) panko breadcrumbs

1½ tbsp plain flour

1½ tbsp harissa paste

1½ tsp tomato purée

1 tsp soy sauce

zest of 1 lemon

1 tbsp chopped coriander leaves

salt and freshly ground black pepper

1 With the wide side of a box grater, grate the squash into a pie or flan dish. Sprinkle on the salt and transfer to a colander for 20 minutes. Press any remaining water out with your hands.

2 In a large frying pan, warm 1 tablespoon of oil over a medium-low heat. Add the onion and cook for 2–3 minutes until soft. Add the garlic and cook for an additional minute. Add the squash and cook for 3–4 minutes. Drain any remaining liquid from the frying pan and transfer the squash to a large mixing bowl. Wipe the frying pan and return to the stove.

3 To the squash mixture, add the red lentils, breadcrumbs, flour, harissa paste, tomato purée, soy sauce, lemon zest, and coriander. Season with salt and pepper to taste.

4 In the frying pan, heat the remaining 2 tablespoons oil over a medium heat. With your hands, form a heaped tablespoon of the squash mixture into a small ball and carefully place in the frying pan. Working in batches, cook the meatballs for 2–3 minutes on each side until lightly browned. Repeat with the remaining mixture. Serve immediately.

Nutrition per meatball

Calories	70
Total Fat	2.5g
Saturated Fat	0g
Cholesterol	0mg
Sodium	170mg
Total Carbohydrate	9g
Dietary Fibre	2g
Sugars	1g
Protein	3g

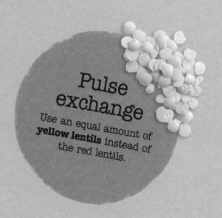

Pulse exchange

Use an equal amount of **yellow lentils** instead of the red lentils.

LENTIL PÂTÉ BANH MI

Creamy lentils replace the traditional meat pâté in this version of the Vietnamese sandwich. Don't skip the sprouted lentils – the texture of these and the crisp vegetables are delightful.

MAKES 4 · PREP 40 MINS · COOK 10 MINS, PLUS 1 HR TO CHILL

325g (11oz) cooked green lentils

60g (2oz) roughly chopped walnuts

1 tbsp miso paste

1 tsp soy sauce or liquid aminos

2 tsp apple cider vinegar

1½ tbsp olive oil

salt and freshly ground black pepper

45g (1½oz) julienned or grated carrot

45g (1½oz) julienned or grated daikon

90ml (3fl oz) rice wine vinegar

pinch of sugar

30g (1oz) sprouted brown lentils

1 long, thin French baguette

85g (3oz) mayonnaise

1 small cucumber, peeled and cut into long strips

2 small jalapeños, thinly sliced

60g (2oz) sprigs of coriander

1 To make the lentil pâté, in a food processor combine the green lentils, walnuts, miso paste, soy sauce, and apple cider vinegar. Blend on low and drizzle in the oil until smooth. Season with salt and pepper to taste. Transfer to a small bowl and cover with cling film, pressing it onto the top of the pâté. Chill in the fridge for 1 hour.

2 In another small bowl, mix together the carrot, daikon, rice wine vinegar, sugar, and sprouted lentils. Toss to coat thoroughly then cover and chill in the fridge for at least 1 hour.

3 Preheat the oven to 180°C (350°F). Horizontally slice through the baguette, leaving the side intact to create a hinge. Then vertically cut fully through the baguette to make 4 equal sections. Place the sections on a baking tray and toast for 5 minutes, or until crispy but not hard. Leave to cool.

4 To assemble the sandwiches, gently open the hinged piece of baguette. Spread equal amounts of mayonnaise inside the top pieces. Spread equal amounts of lentil pâté on the bottom pieces. Top the lentil pâté with the pickled carrot mixture, cucumber, jalapeños, and coriander. Serve the sandwiches immediately.

Make it vegan

Use an egg-free vegan mayonnaise rather than regular mayonnaise.

Make it with meat

Add 30g (1oz) sliced, roasted pork on top of the lentil pâté in each sandwich.

Nutrition per sandwich

Calories	440
Total Fat	24g
Saturated Fat	6g
Cholesterol	15mg
Sodium	760mg
Total Carbohydrate	46g
Dietary Fibre	8g
Sugars	10g
Protein	10g

Why not try...

To make the banh mi heartier, add 30g (1oz) sliced and grilled tofu to each sandwich.

PINTO BEAN & SPIRALIZED SWEET POTATO QUESADILLA

This quesadilla is a great combination of heat from the jalapeño and sweetness from the potato. Spiralizing the sweet potato adds texture to this Mexican snack.

MAKES 4 · PREP 20 MINS · COOK 40 MINS

1 small sweet potato, peeled

2 tbsp vegetable oil

1 jalapeño, deseeded and diced

4 large flour tortillas

225g (8oz) finely grated mature Cheddar cheese

200g (7oz) cooked pinto or borlotti beans

45g (1½oz) chopped spring onion

15g (½oz) chopped coriander leaves

soured cream, to serve

1 With the medium blade of a spiralizer, spiralize the sweet potato.

2 In a medium frying pan, heat the oil over a medium-low heat until shimmering. Add the jalapeño and cook for 3 minutes, or until tender but not brown. Add the sweet potato and cook for 7 minutes, or until just al dente.

3 To assemble, place 1 tortilla on a clean, flat surface. Sprinkle about 28g (1oz) Cheddar on the lower half of the tortilla. Top with ¼ of the pinto beans and ¼ of the sweet potato. Add 2 tablespoons of onion and 2 tablespoons of coriander. Top with another 28g (1oz) Cheddar, then fold over the top of the tortilla to create a semicircle. Repeat to make 4 quesadillas in total.

4 Heat a non-stick frying pan over a medium heat. Add 1 quesadilla and cook for 4 minutes. Carefully turn, cover, and cook for another 4 minutes, until the tortilla is golden and the cheese melted. Repeat for the remaining 3 quesadillas.

5 Cut each quesadilla into 4 sections. Serve immediately with soured cream on the side.

Nutrition per quesadilla

Calories	640
Total Fat	33g
Saturated Fat	17g
Cholesterol	75mg
Sodium	840mg
Total Carbohydrate	61g
Dietary Fibre	9g
Sugars	4g
Protein	26g

● **Make it with meat**

Layer 30g (1oz) cooked, chopped chicken or pork on top of the sweet potato in step 3.

SPICED LENTIL TACOS
WITH GRILLED PINEAPPLE SALSA

Grilling the pineapple in this salsa enhances its already intense sweetness and balances the heat of the jalapeño.

● **Make it with meat**
Add 75g (2½oz) cooked, chopped, smoked pork or turkey to the lentil mixture after removing the bay leaf.

MAKES 8 · PREP 20 MINS · COOK 45 MINS

200g (7oz) uncooked brown lentils

600ml (1 pint) vegetable stock

1 bay leaf

⅛ tsp garlic powder

¼ tsp ground ginger

½ tsp allspice

1½ tsp ground cumin

350g (12oz) fresh pineapple slices

1 small jalapeño, deseeded and finely diced

1 small onion, diced

15g (½oz) chopped coriander leaves

juice of 1 lime

salt and freshly ground black pepper

8 small tortillas

1 In a medium saucepan, combine the lentils, stock, bay leaf, garlic powder, ground ginger, allspice, and cumin. Bring to the boil then reduce to a simmer. Cook over a medium-low heat for 30–35 minutes, until the lentils are tender and most of the stock has been absorbed, adding water as needed. Remove the bay leaf and let sit, covered.

2 Meanwhile, heat a ridged cast-iron grill pan over a medium-high heat. Cook the pineapple slices for 2–3 minutes on each side until caramelized. Remove from the heat and leave to cool.

3 To make the salsa, dice the pineapple and combine in a small mixing bowl with the jalapeño, onion, coriander, and lime juice. Season with salt and pepper to taste.

4 To assemble each taco, place a portion of the lentils onto a tortilla, then top with 2 tablespoons of salsa. Repeat to make 8 tacos in total. Roll the tacos and serve immediately.

Nutrition per taco

Calories	170
Total Fat	1g
Saturated Fat	0g
Cholesterol	0mg
Sodium	55mg
Total Carbohydrate	33g
Dietary Fibre	10g
Sugars	5g
Protein	8g

Pulse exchange
Use an equal amount of **Puy lentils** in place of the brown lentils.

CRISPY AVOCADO & CHICKPEA TACOS

The crispy exterior of the avocado makes a great contrast to the creamy interior. The resulting tacos are juicy and delicious.

MAKES 4 · PREP 25 MINS · COOK 1 HR

300g (10oz) soaked chickpeas

750ml (1¼ pints) vegetable stock

1 tsp garlic powder

1 tbsp ground cumin

1 tbsp ancho chilli powder

1 large egg, beaten

75g (2½oz) panko breadcrumbs

1 tsp chipotle chilli powder

1 large ripe avocado

100g (3½oz) plain Greek-style yogurt

zest and juice of 1 large lime

4 large flour tortillas

75g (2½oz) finely shredded red cabbage

salt and freshly ground black pepper

● Make it vegan

Use 2½ tablespoons of soya milk and 1 tablespoon of ground flaxseed instead of the egg. Replace the yogurt with soya yogurt.

1 In a medium saucepan, combine the chickpeas, stock, and garlic powder. Bring to the boil then reduce to a simmer and cook over a low heat for 1 hour, adding additional water as needed, until the chickpeas are tender. Remove from the heat, drain any excess liquid, and return to the pan. Stir in the cumin and ancho chilli powder. Let sit, covered.

2 Meanwhile, preheat the oven to 180°C (350°F). Arrange two small bowls in your work space. Fill one with egg. In the second, combine the breadcrumbs and chipotle chilli powder. Set up a wire rack on a baking tray.

3 Halve the avocado and remove the pit. Leaving the skin on, cut each half into 4 wedges, making 8 slices. With a flexible spoon or knife, carefully remove the flesh. Dip each slice into the egg and then coat in the breadcrumb mixture, shaking off excess at each stage. Place the slices on the wire rack. Bake for 10–12 minutes, until crisp and lightly golden.

4 In a small bowl, whisk together the yogurt and lime zest and juice. Season with salt and pepper to taste. To prepare each taco, spread 2 tablespoons of yogurt on the tortilla, then add a quarter of the chickpeas, 2 slices of avocado, and a quarter of the cabbage. Roll and serve immediately.

Nutrition per taco

Calories	480
Total Fat	14g
Saturated Fat	2.5g
Cholesterol	50mg
Sodium	510mg
Total Carbohydrate	68g
Dietary Fibre	14g
Sugars	11g
Protein	19g

Pulse exchange

Substitute an equal amount of soaked **black beans** for the chickpeas.

SCARLET RUNNER BURGERS
WITH AVOCADO SALAD

Scarlet Runner beans have a rich, meaty texture, making them perfect for veggie burgers. The creamy avocado and brightness from the lime and coriander balance the richness of the beans.

MAKES 8 · PREP 25 MINS · COOK 15 MINS

1 small onion, finely chopped

2 tbsp olive oil

500g (1lb 2oz) cooked Scarlet Runner beans

1 tsp ground cumin

½ tsp smoked paprika

¼ tsp ground cayenne pepper

1 tsp plain flour

salt and freshly ground black pepper

1 large avocado, diced

1 large red tomato, deseeded and diced

1 small onion, diced

1 small jalapeño, deseeded and diced

2 tbsp chopped coriander leaves

juice of 1 large lime

1 Heat a medium non-stick frying pan over a medium-low heat. Add the oil and heat until warm. Add the finely chopped onion and cook for 2–3 minutes until soft but not brown. Add the garlic and cook for another 1–2 minutes until soft. Remove from the heat and let cool for 5 minutes.

2 In a food processor, combine 420g (15oz) Scarlet Runner beans with the frying pan mixture. Pulse until mashed but not puréed. Transfer to a large mixing bowl and stir in the cumin, paprika, cayenne, flour, and the remaining 80g (3oz) Scarlet Runners. Season with salt and pepper. Chill in the fridge for 15 minutes.

3 Meanwhile, to make the salad, in a small mixing bowl combine the avocado, tomato, the diced onion, jalapeño, coriander, and lime juice. Season with salt to taste. Cover tightly and refrigerate until the burgers are cooked.

4 Lightly oil a medium frying pan over a medium heat. Divide the bean mixture into 8 portions, and form one into a patty with your hands. Place in the frying pan and cook for 4–5 minutes each side until golden brown and holding its shape. Repeat with the remaining bean mixture. Top with the avocado salad and serve immediately.

Nutrition per patty

Calories	170
Total Fat	8g
Saturated Fat	1.5g
Cholesterol	0mg
Sodium	280mg
Total Carbohydrate	21g
Dietary Fibre	8g
Sugars	4g
Protein	8g

Pulse exchange

Instead of Scarlet Runner beans, use 700g (1½lb) **kidney beans**, reserving about 175g (6oz) from the food processor in step 1.

GREEK WHITE BEAN TACOS

This twist on the traditional taco features ingredients typically found in a Greek salad. Romaine lettuce and cucumber add freshness and crunch to the creamy white beans and feta.

MAKES 8 · PREP 25 MINS · COOK 1 HR

2 tbsp olive oil

1 garlic clove, crushed

450g (1lb) cooked haricot beans

zest and juice of 1 large lemon

60ml (2fl oz) vegetable stock

1 tbsp chopped oregano

salt and freshly ground black pepper

100g (3½oz) plain Greek-style yogurt

8 small corn or flour tortillas

85g (3oz) shredded romaine lettuce

350g (12oz) diced plum tomatoes

140g (5oz) diced cucumber

115g (4oz) feta cheese, crumbled

1 In a small casserole or saucepan, heat the oil over a medium-low heat. Add the garlic and cook for 1–2 minutes until soft but not brown. Add the haricot beans, lemon zest and juice, and stock.

2 Bring to a simmer then reduce the heat to low and cook, covered, for 5–6 minutes, until the stock has been absorbed. Stir in the oregano. Season with salt and pepper to taste.

3 To assemble, spread 1 tablespoon of yogurt on a tortilla. Divide the bean mixture into 8 portions and add one portion to the tortilla. Top with a portion of romaine, then tomato, and cucumber. Sprinkle the feta on top. Repeat with the remaining 7 tortillas, fold, and serve immediately.

Nutrition per taco

Calories	210
Total Fat	8g
Saturated Fat	3g
Cholesterol	15mg
Sodium	190mg
Total Carbohydrate	28g
Dietary Fibre	7g
Sugars	3g
Protein	11g

● **Make it with meat**

Add 75g (2½oz) cooked, chopped prawns or chicken along with the beans in step 1.

COURGETTE & BUTTER BEAN FRITTERS

These fritters are light and refreshing, thanks to the lovely green colour and burst of lemon zest. Serve as a side dish with grilled meats or top them with a poached egg and watercress.

MAKES 12 · PREP 20 MINS · COOK 30 MINS

4 medium courgettes

1 tbsp salt

225g (8oz) cooked butter beans

¼ tsp ground cayenne pepper

2 tsp chopped basil leaves

zest of 1 large lemon

2 large eggs, beaten

60g (2oz) panko breadcrumbs

salt and freshly ground black pepper

1 tbsp olive oil

1 With the wide side of a box grater, grate the courgettes. Sprinkle with salt and place in a piece of cheesecloth or kitchen paper. Squeeze to remove as much water as possible and set aside.

2 In a food processor, combine the butter beans, cayenne, basil, lemon zest, and egg. Blend on low for 30–45 seconds until smooth. Transfer to a large mixing bowl and add the courgettes and breadcrumbs. Season with salt and pepper to taste. Stir to combine thoroughly.

3 In a non-stick frying pan, heat the oil over a medium heat. Portion out 4 tablespoons of the bean-courgette mixture, gently form into a ball, and place in the frying pan. With a spatula, lightly press down to form a patty. Working in batches, form the remaining patties and cook for 2–3 minutes on each side until lightly browned. Serve immediately.

● Make it vegan

Use 6 tablespoons water mixed with 2 tablespoons ground flax seeds to replace the egg.

Nutrition per patty

Calories	60
Total Fat	1g
Saturated Fat	0g
Cholesterol	30mg
Sodium	220mg
Total Carbohydrate	10g
Dietary Fibre	2g
Sugars	2g
Protein	4g

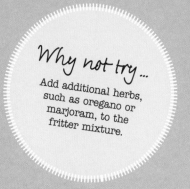

Why not try... Add additional herbs, such as oregano or marjoram, to the fritter mixture.

BAKED FALAFEL
WITH PICKLED RED ONIONS & SAMBAL OELEK

For a healthier version of the Middle Eastern street snack, this falafel is oven-baked instead of fried. Pickled onions and sambal oelek are the perfect tangy-sweet and spicy condiments.

MAKES 16 · PREP 30 MINS, PLUS 3 HRS TO CHILL · COOK 40 MINS

240ml (8fl oz) apple cider vinegar

120ml (4fl oz) red wine vinegar

2 tbsp sugar

1 tsp salt

1 large red onion, thinly sliced

1 garlic clove

350g (12oz) cooked chickpeas

½ tsp bicarbonate of soda

½ tsp ground coriander

½ tsp ground cumin

pinch of crushed dried chillies

1 bunch of curly parsley, chopped

20g (¾oz) finely chopped coriander leaves

zest and juice of 1 lemon

20g (¾oz) chickpea flour

1 tbsp olive oil

75g (2½oz) sambal oelek

1 To make the pickled red onions, in a medium saucepan bring the apple cider vinegar, red wine vinegar, sugar, and salt to the boil over a medium heat. Stir until the sugar and salt dissolve. Remove from the heat and stir in the red onion. Leave to cool completely at room temperature, stirring occasionally. Pour into a glass jar and secure with a lid. Refrigerate for 3 hours or overnight.

2 Preheat the oven to 200°C (400°F). In a food processor, combine the garlic, chickpeas, bicarbonate of soda, ground coriander, cumin, chillies, parsley, chopped coriander, and lemon zest and juice. Pulse until combined but not smooth.

3 Transfer the chickpea mixture to a medium mixing bowl and fold in the chickpea flour. Drizzle oil over and stir once more until it holds together. Season with salt and pepper to taste.

4 Portion out approximately 2 tablespoons of chickpea mixture and roll into a ball with your hands. Place on a baking tray and repeat with the remaining mixture. With a spatula, slightly flatten each one. Bake for 10 minutes, turn over, and bake for an additional 10 minutes. Serve immediately with the pickled red onions and sambal oelek on side.

● **Make it with meat**

Add 225g (8oz) raw minced lamb along with the olive oil in step 3.

Nutrition per patty

Calories	60
Total Fat	1.5g
Saturated Fat	0g
Cholesterol	0mg
Sodium	270mg
Total Carbohydrate	9g
Dietary Fibre	2g
Sugars	2g
Protein	2g

Why not try...

If you'd rather skip the heat, serve with tzatziki sauce instead of spicy sambal.

BRAISED DISHES & CURRIES

CHICKPEA TIKKA MASALA
IN LETTUCE CUPS

Creamy and surprisingly mild, the curry flavour in this dish is a wonderful match for the slightly sweet butterhead lettuce and the textured chickpeas.

SERVES 6 · PREP 20 MINS · COOK 30 MINS

1 tbsp ghee

1 small white onion, chopped

1 tbsp garam masala

½ tsp turmeric

1 small green chilli, deseeded and finely chopped

¼ tsp grated fresh ginger

350g (12oz) cooked chickpeas

500ml (16fl oz) passata

50g (1¾oz) plain Greek-style yogurt

salt and freshly ground black pepper

12 leaves butterhead lettuce, washed and dried

60g (2oz) thinly sliced red onion

2 tbsp chopped coriander leaves

1 In a large frying pan, heat the ghee over a medium-low heat until shimmering. Add the white onion and cook for 2 minutes, or until soft. Add the garam masala, turmeric, chilli, and ginger. Cook for an additional minute to warm the spices.

2 Stir in the chickpeas, passata, and yogurt. Bring to the boil then reduce the heat to low and cook for 20 minutes, or until the sauce and chickpeas are completely warmed through. Season with salt and pepper to taste. Remove from the heat and let sit for 5 minutes.

3 To assemble, divide the chickpea mixture evenly among the leaves. Garnish with the red onion and coriander and serve immediately.

Make it vegan
Replace the ghee with rapeseed oil and the yogurt with coconut milk yogurt.

Make it with meat
Add 125g (4½oz) cooked, chopped chicken breast along with the chickpeas in step 2.

Why not try... For texture and crunch, use Savoy cabbage instead of the butterhead lettuce.

Nutrition per serving

Calories	100
Total Fat	2.5g
Saturated Fat	1g
Cholesterol	<5mg
Sodium	100mg
Total Carbohydrate	15g
Dietary Fibre	4g
Sugars	5g
Protein	5g

GREEN CURRY LENTILS & BROCCOLI

The crunch of broccoli complements the creamy curry sauce, and the lentils introduce another layer of texture to this Thai dish, which is perfect over brown basmati or jasmine rice.

SERVES 8 · PREP 30 MINS · COOK 35 MINS

1 tbsp vegetable oil

1 shallot, finely chopped

1 garlic clove, finely chopped

1 tbsp green curry paste

400 ml (14fl oz) can coconut milk

½ tbsp soy sauce

1 kaffir lime leaf or 1 tbsp fresh lime juice

1 small red pepper, deseeded and julienned

200g (7oz) broccoli florets

325g (11oz) cooked green lentils

100g (3½oz) shiitake mushrooms, sliced

75g (2½oz) chopped fresh green beans

1 tbsp finely chopped basil leaves

salt and freshly ground black pepper

1 In a large saucepan, warm the oil over a medium-low heat until shimmering. Add the shallot and garlic and cook for 2 minutes, or until soft. Add the curry paste and stir to combine. Cook for an additional minute.

2 Add the coconut milk, soy sauce, and kaffir lime leaf or lime juice. Simmer for 10 minutes. Add the red pepper and cook for another 10 minutes, or until the pepper starts to become tender.

3 Stir in the broccoli, lentils, mushrooms, green beans, and basil. Cook for an additional 5–10 minutes, until the green beans and broccoli are tender and the mushrooms are cooked. Remove the kaffir lime leaf, if using. Season with salt and pepper to taste. Serve immediately.

Nutrition per serving

Calories	150
Total Fat	11g
Saturated Fat	9g
Cholesterol	0mg
Sodium	200mg
Total Carbohydrate	11g
Dietary Fibre	4g
Sugars	3g
Protein	4g

● **Make it with meat**

Add 225g (8oz) raw chicken breast, sliced, and cook with the shallots and garlic in step 1.

TOMATO BRAISED WHITE BEANS
WITH GREEN OLIVE POLENTA

These bright, acidic stewed beans served atop creamy polenta make a comforting, filling meal.

SERVES 8 · PREP 20 MINS · COOK 1 HR 40 MINS

1 tbsp olive oil

1 small onion, diced

1 small carrot, diced

1 celery stick, diced

1 garlic clove, finely chopped

1 bay leaf

⅛ tsp crushed dried chillies

1 sprig of rosemary

325g (11oz) soaked cannellini beans

2 x 400g (14oz) cans chopped tomatoes

750–900ml (1¼–1½ pints) vegetable stock

1 litre (1¾ pints) full-fat milk

150g (5½oz) polenta

75g (2½oz) pitted green olives, chopped

salt and freshly ground black pepper

1 In a large flameproof casserole or heavy-based saucepan, heat the oil over a medium-low heat. Add the onion, carrot, and celery and cook for 2–3 minutes until soft. Add the garlic and cook for another 1–2 minutes.

2 Add the bay leaf, crushed chillies, rosemary, cannellini beans, chopped tomatoes, and 240ml (8fl oz) stock. Bring to the boil then reduce to a simmer, and cook over a low heat, covered, for 1 hour, or until the beans are completely tender, adding up to 120ml (4fl oz) stock as needed. Turn off the heat and let sit, covered.

3 To make the polenta, in a medium saucepan bring the remaining 475ml (16fl oz) stock and the milk to the boil then reduce to a simmer. Gradually whisk in the polenta and stir constantly for 5–6 minutes until the mixture thickens. Stir in the olives and cook for an additional minute. Season with salt and pepper to taste.

4 Remove the rosemary stem and bay leaf from the bean mixture. Place the polenta into serving bowls and top with the bean mixture. Serve immediately.

Nutrition per serving

Calories	410
Total Fat	9g
Saturated Fat	3.5g
Cholesterol	15mg
Sodium	430mg
Total Carbohydrate	60g
Dietary Fibre	14g
Sugars	13g
Protein	18g

● **Make it vegan**

Replace the milk with a non-dairy alternative, such as almond milk.

● **Make it with meat**

Stir in 225g (8oz) cooked, crumbled chorizo, once the beans are tender.

Pulse exchange

Use an equal amount of **flageolet beans** instead of the cannellini beans.

RED KIDNEY BEAN CURRY

Meaty kidney beans are simmered in a spicy onion-tomato sauce to create this simple curry, delicous served with basmati rice.

SERVES 6 · PREP 25 MINS · COOK 25 MINS

2 tbsp vegetable oil

1 onion, diced

3 garlic cloves, finely chopped

2 tsp grated fresh ginger

1 small green or red chilli, deseeded and finely chopped

400g (14oz) can chopped tomatoes

¼ tsp turmeric

1 tbsp ground coriander

1 tbsp ground cumin

1 ½ tsp garam masala

500g (1lb 2oz) cooked kidney beans

120ml (4fl oz) vegetable stock

salt and freshly ground black pepper

10g (¼oz) chopped coriander leaves

1 In a heavy-based saucepan or flameproof casserole, heat the oil over a medium-high heat. Add the onion and cook for 2–3 minutes until it begins to soften. Add the garlic, ginger, and chilli and cook for an additional 1–2 minutes.

2 Add the chopped tomatoes, turmeric, ground coriander, cumin, and garam masala. Bring the sauce mixture to the boil then reduce the heat to low and cook, covered, for 7–8 minutes, stirring regularly, until the sauce begins to thicken.

3 Add the kidney beans and stock and cook for an additional 10 minutes, stirring regularly, until the beans are heated through. Season with salt and pepper to taste. Transfer to a serving bowl, garnish with the chopped coriander, and serve immediately.

● **Make it with meat**

Add 225g (8oz) raw, diced chicken breast to the pan before adding the garlic in step 1.

Nutrition per serving

Calories	180
Total Fat	4g
Saturated Fat	3g
Cholesterol	0mg
Sodium	170mg
Total Carbohydrate	28g
Dietary Fibre	9g
Sugars	4g
Protein	9g

Pulse exchange

Use an equal amount of **pinto beans** instead of kidney beans.

DAL BOLOGNESE

There are few dishes more comforting than a classic, slow-cooked Bolognese sauce, used here to create a warmly spiced lentil dish. This is delicious atop rice or polenta.

SERVES 8 · PREP 30 MINS · COOK 1 HR

2 tbsp olive oil

2 celery sticks, finely diced

1 small onion, finely diced

2 carrots, peeled and finely diced

2 garlic cloves, finely chopped

400gm(14oz) uncooked brown lentils

2 x 400g (14oz) cans chopped tomatoes

2 tbsp tomato purée

1 litre (1¾ pints) vegetable stock

1 bay leaf

120ml (4fl oz) double cream

¼ tsp ground nutmeg

salt and freshly ground black pepper

1 In a flameproof casserole or heavy-based saucepan, heat the oil over a medium-low heat until shimmering. Add the celery, onion, and carrot, and cook for 10 minutes, or until tender. Add the garlic and cook for another 3–4 minutes.

2 Add the lentils, tomatoes, tomato purée, stock, and bay leaf. Bring to the boil then reduce the heat to low and simmer, covered, for 35 minutes, or until the lentils are tender and the sauce thickens.

3 Add the double cream and the nutmeg. Stir to combine and cook for an additional 5 minutes. Season with salt and pepper to taste. Remove the bay leaf and serve immediately.

Make it vegan

Substitute soya cream or soya milk for the double cream.

Make it with meat

Add 225g (8oz) raw Italian sausage, minced beef or turkey, along with the celery in step 1.

Nutrition per serving

Calories	290
Total Fat	10g
Saturated Fat	4g
Cholesterol	20mg
Sodium	180mg
Total Carbohydrate	39g
Dietary Fibre	17g
Sugars	7g
Protein	14g

Pulse exchange

Use an equal amount of **green lentils** in place of the brown lentils.

DAL MAKHANI

These buttery lentils are rich and spicy. Serve this Indian recipe with warm naan to soak up the luscious sauce.

SERVES 4 · PREP 20 MINS · COOK 1 HR

2 tbsp ghee or vegetable oil

1 garlic clove, finely chopped

1½ tsp grated fresh ginger

1 small green chilli, deseeded and finely chopped

1¼ tsp turmeric

1¼ tsp ground coriander

350g (12oz) passata

120ml (4fl oz) water

450g (1lb) cooked black lentils

80ml (3fl oz) double cream

salt

10g (¼oz) chopped coriander leaves

1 In a medium stock pot, warm the ghee over a medium-low heat until shimmering. Add the garlic, ginger, and chilli and cook for 2–3 minutes until soft. Stir in the turmeric and ground coriander.

2 Stir in the passata, water, and black lentils. Cook, uncovered, for 5–6 minutes until the liquid reduces and thickens slightly.

3 Gradually stir in the double cream. Simmer, uncovered, over a low heat for another 10 minutes. Season with salt to taste. Garnish with chopped coriander and serve immediately.

Nutrition per serving

Calories	430
Total Fat	20g
Saturated Fat	11g
Cholesterol	45mg
Sodium	200mg
Total Carbohydrate	49g
Dietary Fibre	10g
Sugars	8g
Protein	16g

●Make it vegan

Use an equal amount of coconut milk in place of the double cream.

WHITE BEAN COCONUT CURRY

This spicy curry is super creamy thanks to the smooth haricot beans and the rich sauce.

SERVES 6 · PREP 25 MINS · COOK 35 MINS

1 tbsp coconut oil

1 small onion, diced

1 orange or yellow pepper, diced

1 garlic clove, finely chopped

1 tsp grated fresh ginger

2 tbsp red curry paste

2 tbsp tomato purée

1 tsp ground coriander

½ tsp garam masala

¼ tsp turmeric

400ml (14fl oz) can coconut milk

675g (1½lb) cooked haricot beans

15g (½oz) chopped coriander leaves

1 In a heavy-based saucepan, heat the oil over a medium-low heat until shimmering. Add the onion and pepper and cook for 2 minutes until soft. Add the garlic and ginger and cook for 2 minutes.

2 Stir in the red curry paste, tomato purée, ground coriander, garam masala, and turmeric. Cook for 1 minute to warm the spices. Pour in the coconut milk and stir to combine.

3 Add the haricot beans and bring to the boil, reduce the heat and simmer, covered, for 20 minutes, or until the sauce thickens and the beans are warmed through. Garnish with chopped coriander and serve immediately.

Nutrition per serving

Calories	280
Total Fat	14g
Saturated Fat	11g
Cholesterol	0mg
Sodium	160mg
Total Carbohydrate	31g
Dietary Fibre	11g
Sugars	3g
Protein	9g

●Make it with meat

Sauté 225g (8oz) peeled and de-veined prawns with butter and garlic and serve atop the dish.

CAJUN BRAISED BLACK-EYED BEANS

Vinegar and spicy cayenne balance earthy black-eyed beans for a Southern Creole flavour. Serve this brothy recipe with brown rice or quinoa for a filling meal.

SERVES 4 · PREP 15 MINS · COOK 50 MINS

1 tbsp rapeseed or
   vegetable oil

1 green pepper, finely diced

1 onion, finely diced

1 celery stick, finely diced

1 garlic clove, finely chopped

5 sprigs of thyme

1 bay leaf

600ml (1 pint) vegetable stock

250g (9oz) soaked black-eyed
   beans

¾ tsp ground cayenne pepper

½ tsp paprika

1 tbsp white wine vinegar

salt and freshly ground
   black pepper

1 In a medium casserole or heavy-based saucepan, heat the oil over a medium-low heat. Add the pepper, onion, and celery. Cook for 3–4 minutes until soft. Add the garlic and cook for an additional 1–2 minutes.

2 Add the thyme, bay leaf, and the stock. Bring to the boil then reduce the heat and simmer for 5 minutes. Stir in the black-eyed beans, cayenne, and paprika.

3 Bring to the boil then reduce the heat to low and cook, covered, for 30–40 minutes until the beans are tender. Add up to 120ml (4fl oz) additional stock or water as needed.

4 Stir in the vinegar and season with salt and pepper to taste. Remove the thyme stems and bay leaf. Serve immediately.

● **Make it with meat**

Add 75g (2½oz) cooked, diced ham or smoked pork to the braising liquid, along with the beans.

Pulse exchange

Use 140g (5oz) soaked **pigeon peas** instead of black-eyed beans.

Nutrition per serving

Calories	270
Total Fat	5g
Saturated Fat	0g
Cholesterol	0mg
Sodium	780mg
Total Carbohydrate	41g
Dietary Fibre	11g
Sugars	5g
Protein	13g

BRAISED LEEKS & PUY LENTILS

Simple to make yet sophisticated in flavour, braising leeks brings out their subtle sweetness and contrasts beautifully with the earthy flavour of Puy lentils.

SERVES 6 · PREP 15 MINS · COOK 30 MINS

6 leeks
3 tbsp unsalted butter
1 tbsp dry vermouth
3 sprigs of thyme
120ml (4fl oz) vegetable stock
325g (11oz) cooked Puy or green lentils
salt and freshly ground black pepper
2 tbsp chopped flat-leaf parsley

1 Carefully trim and remove the root from the leeks while keeping them intact. Cut off the dark green tops and remove the tough outer layers. Cut each leek in half lengthways. Submerge in cold water for 5 minutes to remove any dirt from inside. Transfer to a colander to drain.

2 In a 30cm (12in) frying pan, melt the butter over a medium-low heat. Add the vermouth. Place the leeks cut-side down in the frying pan and cook for 4 minutes.

3 Add the thyme and stock. Bring to a gentle boil then reduce to a simmer. Cook, covered, for 10–15 minutes until the leeks are tender.

4 Add the lentils and cook for an additional 5 minutes. Season with salt and pepper to taste.

5 Remove the thyme stems. With tongs, transfer the leeks to a serving platter. Pour the lentils and cooking liquid over the leeks. Garnish with the parsley and serve immediately.

Make it vegan

Replace the unsalted butter with a vegan butter alternative.

Make it with meat

Instead of butter, use the melted fat from frying 6 chopped rashers of bacon, then proceed with the vermouth in step 2, leaving the bacon bits in the pan.

Pulse exchange

Instead of green lentils, use an equal amount of **black lentils** or **moth beans.**

Nutrition per serving

Calories	150
Total Fat	6g
Saturated Fat	3g
Cholesterol	15mg
Sodium	20mg
Total Carbohydrate	19g
Dietary Fibre	4g
Sugars	4g
Protein	4g

BRAISED BUTTER & HARICOT BEANS
WITH CHERMOULA

Originating in North Africa, chermoula is a tart, herby sauce. Its punchy flavour and bright colour provide a tasty complement to creamy braised beans.

SERVES 6 · PREP 35 MINS · COOK 30 MINS

20g (¾oz) roughly chopped parsley

60g (2oz) roughly chopped coriander leaves

5 garlic cloves

1 tbsp smoked paprika

1½ tsp ground cumin

2 tbsp cold water

2 tbsp lemon juice

75ml (2½fl oz) olive oil

1 small onion, diced

1 celery stick, diced

1 large carrot, diced

1 bay leaf

4 sprigs of thyme

600ml (1 pint) vegetable stock

325g (11oz) cooked butter beans

450g (1lb) cooked haricot beans

1 To make the chermoula, in a food processor combine the parsley, coriander, 4 garlic cloves, paprika, cumin, water, and lemon juice. Process on low. With the processor running, drizzle in 60ml (2fl oz) oil. Blend until smooth. Transfer the contents to a small bowl and cover with cling film, pressing onto the top of the sauce so it does not oxidize. Refrigerate until ready to serve.

2 In a medium flameproof casserole or heavy-based saucepan, heat the remaining 1 tablespoon oil over a medium-low heat until warm. Add the onion, celery, and carrot. Cook for 2–3 minutes until soft. Crush the remaining garlic clove and add to the vegetables. Cook for an additional minute.

3 Add the bay leaf, thyme, stock, butter beans, and haricot beans. Bring to the boil then reduce the heat to low and cook, covered, for 20 minutes, or until the liquid thickens and the beans are warmed through. Season with salt and pepper to taste.

4 Remove the bay leaf and thyme stems. Serve immediately with the chermoula on the side.

Nutrition per serving

Calories	250
Total Fat	8g
Saturated Fat	1g
Cholesterol	0mg
Sodium	85mg
Total Carbohydrate	36g
Dietary Fibre	13g
Sugars	4g
Protein	11g

MOROCCAN SQUASH & PIGEON PEA TAGINE

● **Make it with meat**

Brown 450g (1lb) lamb shoulder, diced, and add with the squash.

This slow-cooked, warmly spiced squash stew receives its name from the earthenware pot in which it's traditionally cooked, but you can create the same depth of flavour without a tagine.

SERVES 6 · PREP 45 MINS · COOK 40 MINS

1 tbsp coconut oil

1 onion, chopped

1 carrot, diced

2 garlic cloves, finely chopped

1 tsp grated fresh ginger

1 tsp smoked paprika

1 cinnamon stick

¼ tsp allspice

½ tsp ground coriander

¼ tsp ground cardamom

2 tbsp tomato purée

475ml (16fl oz) vegetable stock

1 large acorn or butternut squash, peeled, deseeded, and diced, about 675g (1½lb)

325g (11oz) cooked pigeon peas

juice of 1 large lemon

75g (2½oz) pitted and chopped dates

1 In a tagine or large flameproof casserole, heat the coconut oil over a medium-low heat. Add the onion and carrot and cook for 2–3 minutes. Add the garlic and ginger and cook, uncovered, for an additional 1–2 minutes.

2 Add the paprika, cinnamon stick, allspice, ground coriander, and cardamom. Cook for 1 minute to warm the spices. Add the tomato purée and stock and stir to combine.

3 Stir in the squash and simmer, covered, for 15 minutes. Add the pigeon peas and cook for an additional 10 minutes, or until the squash is tender and the peas are warmed through. Stir in the lemon juice and dates. Season with salt and pepper to taste. Remove the cinnamon stick and serve immediately.

Nutrition per serving

Calories	210
Total Fat	2.5g
Saturated Fat	2g
Cholesterol	0mg
Sodium	260mg
Total Carbohydrate	41g
Dietary Fibre	8g
Sugars	22g
Protein	5g

Pulse exchange

For a traditional tagine, substitute an equal amount of **chickpeas** for the pigeon peas.

INDIAN SPICED SPINACH & LENTILS

Inspired by Indian *saag* dishes, this recipe incorporates green lentils to add texture to a creamy spinach dish. Serve with warm garlic naan and rice for a complete meal.

SERVES 4 · PREP 15 MINS · COOK 30 MINS

1½ tsp cumin seeds

6 tbsp ghee

1½ tsp turmeric

½ tsp ground coriander

1 large green chilli, deseeded and finely chopped

2 garlic cloves, finely chopped

675g (1½lb) baby spinach

450g (1lb) cooked green lentils

60ml (2fl oz) double cream

salt and freshly ground black pepper

1 With a mortar and pestle, grind the cumin seeds into a fine powder to release their fragrance.

2 In a heavy-based saucepan, heat the ghee over a medium-low heat until shimmering. Add the cumin, turmeric, and ground coriander and cook for 1 minute. Add the chilli and cook for 3 minutes, or until it begins to soften. Add the garlic and cook for an additional 2 minutes.

3 Add the spinach and stir to combine. Cook for 5 minutes, or until the spinach begins to wilt.

4 Stir in the green lentils and double cream. Simmer, partially covered, over a low heat for 15 minutes, stirring regularly, or until the spinach is cooked and the sauce thickens.

5 Season with salt and pepper to taste. Serve immediately.

Make it vegan

Replace the ghee with rapeseed or vegetable oil and use a non-dairy cream alternative.

Make it with meat

Add 125g (4½oz) cooked, chopped chicken breast along with the lentils in step 4.

Pulse exchange

Substitute 175g (6oz) cooked **mung beans** for the green lentils.

Nutrition per serving

Calories	420
Total Fat	11g
Saturated Fat	7g
Cholesterol	10mg
Sodium	135mg
Total Carbohydrate	57g
Dietary Fibre	32g
Sugars	<1g
Protein	24g

PIGEON PEA VINDALOO

Characteristic of vindaloo, the high heat level in this Indian curry balances with warm spices, such as cinnamon and cardamom. Serve with rice or naan and some cooling yogurt raita.

SERVES 4 · PREP 25 MINS · COOK 35 MINS

1¼ tbsp ground cumin

1 tbsp ground coriander

¾ tsp turmeric

⅔ tsp ground cardamom

½ tbsp ground mustard seeds

1 tbsp paprika

1 tbsp vegetable oil

1 small onion, diced

3 garlic cloves, finely chopped

¾ tbsp finely chopped fresh ginger

1 large hot red chilli, deseeded and finely chopped

1 bay leaf

1 cinnamon stick

225g (8oz) passata

1 tbsp red wine vinegar

240ml (8fl oz) water

450g (1lb) cooked pigeon peas, or black-eyed beans

salt and freshly ground black pepper

1 In a small bowl, combine the cumin, ground coriander, turmeric, cardamom, mustard, and paprika and stir thoroughly to combine.

2 In a heavy-bottomed pan, heat the oil over a medium heat until shimmering. Add the onion and cook for 3–4 minutes until it starts to become translucent.

3 Stir in the garlic, ginger, and chilli, and cook for an additional 2 minutes. Incorporate the spice mixture, bay leaf, cinnamon stick, passata, vinegar, and water, and bring to the boil. Reduce the heat and simmer, covered, for 10 minutes.

4 Add the pigeon peas (or black-eyed beans) and stir to combine. Bring to the boil then reduce to a simmer and cook, covered, for 20 minutes. Remove the cinnamon stick and bay leaf. Season with salt and pepper to taste. Serve immediately.

Nutrition per serving

Calories	250
Total Fat	5g
Saturated Fat	3g
Cholesterol	0mg
Sodium	590mg
Total Carbohydrate	42g
Dietary Fibre	12g
Sugars	9g
Protein	11g

● **Make it with meat**

Brown 450g (1lb) chuck steak, diced, and add with the passata.

CURRIED SQUASH & MUNG BEAN DOPIAZA

The pronounced flavours of the caramelized onion and lightly sautéed onion combine with creamy coconut to create this *dopiaza*, which means "two onions".

SERVES 6 · PREP 30 MINS · COOK 55 MINS

675g (1½lb) peeled and diced butternut squash

2 tbsp vegetable oil

2 onions

2 garlic cloves, finely chopped

1 tsp grated fresh ginger

1½ tsp ground cumin

1 tsp ground coriander

2¼ tsp garam masala

1 tsp crushed dried chillies

½ tsp turmeric

60g (2oz) passata

400ml (14fl oz) can coconut milk

3 plum tomatoes, roughly chopped

240ml (8fl oz) vegetable stock

500g (1lb 2oz) cooked mung beans

10g (¼oz) chopped coriander leaves

1 Preheat the oven to 190°C (375°F). Toss the squash with 1 tablespoon of oil and spread in an even layer on a baking tray. Roast for 15–25 minutes until tender, stirring occasionally.

2 Meanwhile, dice one onion and thinly slice the other onion. Set aside in separate bowls.

3 In a large saucepan, heat the remaining 1 tablespoon of oil over a medium-low heat until shimmering. To caramelize the sliced onion, add to the saucepan and cook for 7–8 minutes until golden brown. Remove from the pan and set aside.

4 Add the diced onion to the pan and cook for 2–3 minutes until soft. Add the garlic and ginger and cook for an additional 1–2 minutes. Stir in the cumin, ground coriander, garam masala, crushed dried chillies, and turmeric, and cook for 1 minute to heat the spices.

5 Pour in the passata, coconut milk, tomatoes, and stock. Bring to the boil then reduce to a simmer and cook for 5 minutes, or until the ingredients are incorporated and the tomatoes are tender. Remove from the heat and leave to cool.

6 Pour the tomato mixture into a blender and purée until smooth. Transfer the sauce back to the pan and warm over a medium-low heat. Add the roasted squash and mung beans. Simmer for 15 minutes, covered, or until the sauce thickens slightly. Stir in the caramelized sliced onions. Garnish with the chopped coriander and serve immediately.

● **Make it with meat**

Reduce the squash by a quarter and add 125g (4½oz) cooked, chopped chicken breast to the pan along with squash.

Nutrition per serving

Calories	320
Total Fat	17g
Saturated Fat	14g
Cholesterol	0mg
Sodium	65mg
Total Carbohydrate	37g
Dietary Fibre	9g
Sugars	8g
Protein	10g

BRAISED WHITE BEANS
WITH SPINACH & POMEGRANATE

Creamy beans contrast with cool, crunchy pomegranate seeds in this dish. The seeds are added only at the end to prevent it turning pink!

SERVES 6 · PREP 20 MINS · COOK 30 MINS

1 tbsp olive oil

1 small onion, diced

1 garlic clove, finely chopped

3 sprigs of thyme

60ml (2fl oz) dry white wine

475ml (16fl oz) vegetable stock

500g (1lb 2oz) cooked cannellini beans

85g (3oz) baby spinach

salt and freshly ground black pepper

15g (½oz) finely grated Parmesan cheese

60g (2oz) pomegranate seeds

1 In a medium flameproof casserole or heavy-based saucepan, heat the oil over a medium-low heat until shimmering. Add the onion and cook for 2–3 minutes until soft. Add the garlic and cook for an additional 1–2 minutes.

2 Stir in the thyme, wine, and stock. Bring to the boil then reduce to a simmer. Add the cannellini beans and return to the boil. Then reduce the heat and simmer again, covered, stirring occasionally, for 20 minutes, or until the liquid reduces slightly and the beans are heated through.

3 Remove the lid, stir in the spinach, and cook over a medium-low heat, uncovered, for 4–5 minutes. Season with salt and pepper to taste.

4 Remove from the heat, remove the thyme stems, and stir in the Parmesan. Sprinkle the pomegranate seeds on top and serve immediately.

● Make it vegan

Replace the Parmesan with an equal amount of nutritional yeast.

● Make it with meat

For a deeper flavour, add 30g (1oz) diced pancetta along with the onion.

Pulse exchange

Instead of cannellini beans, use an equal amount of **flageolet beans**.

Nutrition per serving

Calories	180
Total Fat	4g
Saturated Fat	1g
Cholesterol	<5mg
Sodium	120mg
Total Carbohydrate	24g
Dietary Fibre	7g
Sugars	4g
Protein	10g

SWEET & SOUR CABBAGE
WITH BROWN LENTILS

This is a simple version of a German classic. Sugar, apple, and vinegar combine for a smooth flavour that's even more delicious when reheated the next day – so set some aside for tomorrow's lunch.

SERVES 4 · PREP 20 MINS · COOK 50 MINS

1 tbsp olive oil

1 shallot, finely chopped

1 head of red cabbage, core removed, shredded

1 small Granny Smith apple, peeled and thinly sliced

¼ tsp fennel seeds

3 tbsp light brown sugar

120ml (4fl oz) apple cider vinegar

125g (4½oz) cooked brown lentils

1 In a flameproof casserole or heavy-based saucepan, warm the oil over a medium heat. Add the shallot and cook for 3 minutes, or until soft but not brown. Add the cabbage and apple and stir to combine.

2 Add the fennel seeds, brown sugar, and vinegar. Bring to the boil then reduce the heat to low and simmer, covered, for 25 minutes.

3 Add the lentils, stir thoroughly, and re-cover. Cook for an additional 20 minutes, or until the cabbage is tender and the lentils are warmed through. Serve immediately.

Nutrition per serving

Calories	210
Total Fat	4g
· Saturated Fat	0g
Cholesterol	0mg
Sodium	60mg
Total Carbohydrate	41g
Dietary Fibre	9g
Sugars	23g
Protein	8g

● **Make it with meat**

Add 2 rashers raw, chopped bacon and cook alongside the shallot in step 1.

BRAISED CHICKPEAS
WITH PRESERVED LEMON

A North African condiment, these lemon slices preserved in brine add a fragrant touch to a simply braised chickpea and chard recipe.

SERVES 6 · PREP 15 MINS · COOK 35 MINS

1 tbsp olive oil

1 small onion, chopped

1 garlic clove, finely chopped

500g (1lb 2oz) cooked chickpeas

450g (1lb) chopped Swiss chard, leaves and stems

120ml (4fl oz) vegetable stock

75g (2½ oz) chopped green olives

½ tbsp finely chopped preserved lemon, or zest and juice of 1 lemon

salt and freshly ground black pepper

1 In a large flameproof casserole, warm the oil over a medium heat until shimmering. Add the onion and cook for 2 minutes, or until soft. Add the garlic and cook for an additional minute.

2 Add the chickpeas and Swiss chard and stir to combine. Add the stock and cook, covered, for 15 minutes, or until the chard begins to wilt.

3 Stir in the olives and preserved lemon. Cook, covered, for an additional 10 minutes. Season with salt and pepper to taste. Serve immediately.

Pulse exchange
Use an equal amount of **cannellini beans** instead of the chickpeas.

Nutrition per serving

Calories	190
Total Fat	6g
Saturated Fat	1g
Cholesterol	0mg
Sodium	530mg
Total Carbohydrate	29g
Dietary Fibre	8g
Sugars	7g
Protein	9g

LENTIL & TOMATO BRAISED GREEN BEANS

The secret of this dish is in the yellow tomatoes – they have an acidity that brightens the entire recipe. You'll be surprised at the depth of flavour achieved from such a simple braise.

SERVES 6 · PREP 15 MINS · COOK 1 HR 10 MINS, PLUS 5 MINS TO COOL

350g (12oz) green beans

1 tbsp olive oil

1 small onion, finely diced

1 garlic clove, finely chopped

25–30 golden cherry
  tomatoes, halved

60ml (2fl oz) dry white wine

350ml (12fl oz) vegetable
  stock

pinch of crushed dried
  chillies

85g (3oz) cooked brown lentils

salt and freshly ground
  black pepper

1 Trim the ends from the green beans. Rinse and drain. In a medium flameproof casserole or heavy-based saucepan, heat the oil over a medium-low heat. Add the onion and cook for 2–3 minutes until soft. Add the garlic and cook for an additional 1–2 minutes.

2 Add the cherry tomatoes and white wine. Stir to combine and cook, covered, for 5 minutes. Add the stock and dried chillies. Bring to the boil then reduce to a simmer and cook, covered, for 15 minutes, stirring occasionally.

3 Add the green beans. Return to a simmer and cook, covered, for 10 minutes. Add the brown lentils and cook, covered, for 30 minutes, or until the green beans are tender and the liquid thickens. Season with salt and pepper to taste.

4 Remove from the heat and let sit, covered, for 5–10 minutes to let any remaining liquid thicken before serving.

● **Make it with meat**

For a salty, smoky flavour, cook 30g (1oz) pancetta along with the onion.

Nutrition per serving

Calories	140
Total Fat	2.5g
Saturated Fat	0g
Cholesterol	0mg
Sodium	40mg
Total Carbohydrate	21g
Dietary Fibre	9g
Sugars	5g
Protein	7g

Pulse exchange

Substitute an equal amount of cooked **Puy** or **green lentils** for the brown lentils.

FRIJOLES BORRACHOS

This Mexican recipe translates to "drunken beans" – a savoury, soupy, and scrumptious all-purpose dish.

SERVES 8 · PREP 20 MINS · COOK 1 HR 30 MINS

2 litres (3½ pints) vegetable stock

450g (1lb) dry pinto beans, soaked

1 large onion, halved

3 garlic cloves

1 tbsp vegetable oil

1 small Serrano chilli, deseeded and finely chopped

2 large tomatoes, chopped

350ml (12fl oz) dark Mexican beer

2 tbsp tomato purée

salt and freshly ground black pepper

1 In a large stock pot, combine the stock, pinto beans, 1 onion half, and 1 garlic clove. Bring to the boil then reduce to a simmer over a medium heat and cook, covered, for 45 minutes to 1 hour, until the beans are tender, adding additional stock as needed.

2 Meanwhile, dice the remaining onion half and finely chop the remaining 2 garlic cloves.

3 Remove the pot from heat, drain the beans into a colander, and remove the garlic clove and large onion pieces. Set the beans aside and leave to dry.

4 Wipe out the pot. Add the oil and return the pot to the stove over a medium-low heat. Add the diced onion and cook for 2–3 minutes until soft. Add the chopped garlic and chilli and cook for an additional minute.

5 Add the pinto beans, tomatoes, beer, and tomato purée. Stir to combine. Simmer, covered, for 20 minutes, or until the beer cooks off and the liquid thickens slightly. Season with salt and pepper to taste. Serve immediately.

Nutrition per serving

Calories	270
Total Fat	2.5g
Saturated Fat	1.5g
Cholesterol	0mg
Sodium	430mg
Total Carbohydrate	45g
Dietary Fibre	11g
Sugars	6g
Protein	13g

Pulse exchange
450g (1lb) dry **kidney beans** or **borlotti beans**, soaked, are a good substitute for pinto beans.

BAKED DISHES & CASSEROLES

CURRIED BLACK LENTIL STUFFED ONIONS

The nuttiness of black lentils and quinoa mixed with creamy goat's cheese makes these onions a unique main course.

● **Make it with meat**

Reduce the cooked black lentils to 100g (3½oz) and add 225g (8oz) cooked minced lamb along with the lentils.

MAKES 8 · PREP 30 MINS · COOK 1 HR

4 onions

240ml (8fl oz) water

550ml (18fl oz) vegetable stock

½ tsp curry powder

½ tsp garam masala

175g (6oz) uncooked red, black, and white quinoa

140g (5oz) cooked black lentils

175g (6oz) crumbled goat's cheese

10g (¼oz) plus 2 tbsp chopped coriander leaves

salt and freshly ground black pepper

1 Preheat the oven to 190°C (375°F). Trim both ends off the onions and discard the skins. Cut each onion horizontally in half to create 2 flat sections. To create a well for the filling, with a spoon or melon baller gently scoop out the middle of each onion half, leaving the bottom of the onion intact.

2 Arrange the onions in a 20 × 20cm (8 × 8in) glass or ceramic baking dish, well-side up, and fill the bottom of the dish with water. Cover the dish with foil and bake for 40 minutes, or until the onions are tender.

3 Meanwhile, in a medium saucepan, combine the stock, curry powder, and garam masala. Bring gradually to the boil and add the dry quinoa. Return to the boil then reduce to a simmer and cook, covered, for 15–18 minutes until tender. Remove from the heat and let sit, covered, for 5 minutes.

4 In a large mixing bowl, combine the cooked and seasoned quinoa, black lentils, goat's cheese, and 10g (¼oz) coriander. Thoroughly combine. Season with salt and pepper to taste.

5 Spoon an equal amount of quinoa mixture into each onion half. Bake, uncovered, for 20 minutes, or until the filling is toasted and warmed through. Garnish with the remaining 2 tablespoons of coriander and serve immediately.

Nutrition per onion half

Calories	240
Total Fat	7g
Saturated Fat	3.5g
Cholesterol	10mg
Sodium	140mg
Total Carbohydrate	30g
Dietary Fibre	6g
Sugars	4g
Protein	12g

MOTH BEAN STUFFED SWEET POTATOES
WITH BRIE & POMEGRANATE

The surprising mix of sweet and savoury in these baked potatoes makes for a truly luscious vegetarian meal or hearty side dish.

MAKES 8 · PREP 15 MINS · COOK 1 HR 15 MINS

4 sweet potatoes, about 1kg (2lb) in total

500g (1lb 2oz) cooked moth beans, or black lentils

225g (8oz) Brie

salt and freshly ground black pepper

175g (6oz) pomegranate seeds

30g (1oz) roughly chopped coriander leaves

1 Preheat the oven to 220°C (425°F) and line a baking tray with foil.

2 Cut each potato in half lengthways. Lightly oil each cut side. Arrange the potatoes cut-side down on the baking tray and bake for 30–40 minutes until tender all the way through.

3 To assemble, turn the sweet potato halves cut-side up. With a fork, fluff the inside of the potatoes while keeping the skin intact. Top each potato half with an equal amount of moth beans (or lentils) and an equal amount of Brie. Season with salt and pepper.

4 Bake for an additional 8–10 minutes until the Brie is melted and gooey. Sprinkle each potato half with 2 tablespoons of pomegranate seeds and 2 tablespoons of chopped coriander. Serve immediately.

Nutrition per sweet potato half

Calories	320
Total Fat	9g
Saturated Fat	5g
Cholesterol	30mg
Sodium	210mg
Total Carbohydrate	48g
Dietary Fibre	6g
Sugars	16g
Protein	15g

● **Make it with meat**

Crumble 60g (2oz) cooked cripy bacon into each potato, along with the pomegranate seeds.

ASIAN ADZUKI BAKED BEANS

The flavour of these beans is reminiscent of Korean barbecue – sweet and savoury, with gentle heat from the Gochujang.

SERVES 8 · PREP 20 MINS · COOK 1 HR 5 MINS

1 tbsp sesame oil

1 onion, diced

1 tbsp tomato purée

100g (3½oz) light brown sugar

2½ tbsp molasses

1½ tsp ground mustard seeds

½ tsp ground ginger

2 tbsp Gochujang

1 tbsp rice wine vinegar

1 tbsp light soy sauce

1.25kg (2¾lb) cooked adzuki beans

180ml (6fl oz) vegetable stock

salt and freshly ground black pepper

1 Preheat the oven to 180°C (325°F). In a large frying pan, heat the sesame oil over a medium-low heat. Add the onion and cook for 2–3 minutes until soft. Add the tomato purée, brown sugar, molasses, mustard, ground ginger, Gochujang, vinegar, and soy sauce. Cook for 2–3 minutes until the mixture bubbles.

2 Stir in the adzuki beans. Transfer the mixture to a 2-litre (3½-pint) glass baking dish. Pour in the stock and mix gently. Cover the dish with foil and cook for 30 minutes. Remove the foil and cook for an additional 20 minutes, or until thickened. Serve immediately.

Nutrition per serving

Calories	320
Total Fat	2g
Saturated Fat	0g
Cholesterol	0mg
Sodium	220mg
Total Carbohydrate	62g
Dietary Fibre	13g
Sugars	20g
Protein	14g

● Make it with meat

For a smoky flavour, chop 2 rashers of bacon and cook with the onions in step 1.

GREEK STUFFED TOMATOES

Dill and mint are tasty in stuffed tomatoes, served here with their lids on.

MAKES 6 · PREP 30 MINS · COOK 4 HR

6 large red tomatoes

180ml (6fl oz) veg stock

3 tbsp olive oil

1 small onion, finely diced

2 garlic cloves, minced

2 tbsp tomato purée

10g (¼oz) chopped dill

10g (¼oz) chopped mint

5g (⅛oz) chopped flat-leaf parsley

zest and juice of 1 lemon

225g (8oz) cooked haricot beans

150g (5½oz) cooked brown basmati rice

salt and pepper

1 Preheat the oven to 200°C (400°F). Cut the top quarter off the tomatoes, set aside, and scoop out the flesh. Place in a baking dish. Pour 120ml (4fl oz) stock into the dish.

2 In a large frying pan, heat 1 tablespoon oil over a medium-low heat. Add the onion and cook for 2–3 minutes. Add the garlic and cook for 1 minute. Stir in the tomato purée, dill, mint, parsley, lemon zest and juice, remaining stock, haricot beans, and rice. Season with salt and pepper.

3 Divide the filling among the tomatoes and replace tops. Drizzle with the remaining oil. Cover with foil and cook for 20 minutes. Remove the foil and cook for an additional 20 minutes, or until tender. Serve immediately.

Nutrition per tomato

Calories	180
Total Fat	8g
Saturated Fat	1g
Cholesterol	0mg
Sodium	400mg
Total Carbohydrate	26g
Dietary Fibre	6g
Sugars	7g
Protein	5g

● Make it with meat

Reduce the haricot beans by half and stir 75g (2½oz) cooked minced lamb or beef into the stuffing.

GREEN SPLIT PEA STUFFED CABBAGE

Cuisines from all over the world feature inspired versions of stuffed cabbage. This recipe uses green split peas for added texture in the filling.

● **Make it with meat**

Omit 60g (2oz) cooked brown rice and add 225g (8oz) cooked minced lamb or beef to the rice mixture.

MAKES 15 · PREP 50 MINS · COOK 1 HR 5 MINS

1 small head of Savoy cabbage

2 tbsp olive oil

1 small onion, diced

1 garlic clove, finely chopped

¼ tsp crushed dried chillies

1 bay leaf

2 sprigs of thyme

2 x 400g (14oz) cans chopped tomatoes

120ml (4fl oz) vegetable stock

1 tbsp balsamic vinegar

salt and freshly ground black pepper

225g (8oz) cooked brown rice

325g (11oz) cooked green split peas

60g (2oz) chopped, pitted green olives

30g (1oz) toasted chopped walnuts

zest and juice of 1 lemon

pinch of cinnamon

Nutrition per cabbage leaf

Calories	120
Total Fat	4g
Saturated Fat	0g
Cholesterol	0mg
Sodium	140mg
Total Carbohydrate	20g
Dietary Fibre	6g
Sugars	5g
Protein	5g

1 Preheat the oven to 175°C (375°F). Bring a large pan of water to the boil. Cut the core out of the cabbage and select 15 leaves to stuff. With a paring knife, carefully remove the hard stem of each leaf. Blanch the leaves for 1–2 minutes until bright green and tender. Leave to dry on kitchen paper.

2 In a medium saucepan, heat 1½ tablespoons of oil over a medium-low heat. Add the onion and cook for 2–3 minutes until soft. Add the garlic and cook for an additional minute. Stir in the crushed dried chillies, bay leaf, thyme, tomatoes, stock, and vinegar. Bring to the boil then reduce to a simmer and cook for 10–12 minutes. Season with salt and pepper to taste. Remove the bay leaf and thyme stems.

3 Meanwhile, heat a large frying pan over a medium-low heat. Add the remaining ½ tablespoon oil and warm until shimmering. Add the brown rice, green split peas, olives, walnuts, lemon zest and juice, and cinnamon. Cook over a low heat for 10 minutes, or until warmed through. Season with salt and pepper to taste.

4 Coat the bottom of a 23 x 33cm (9 x 13in) baking dish with some of the tomato sauce mixture. Take one cabbage leaf and place it on a clean, flat work surface. Place about 5 tablespoons rice filling on top of the leaf and roll into a small bundle. Place seam-side down in the dish. Repeat with the remaining leaves and filling. Cover the stuffed cabbage evenly with the remaining tomato sauce mixture.

5 Cover the dish with foil and bake for 20 minutes. Remove the foil and cook for another 15–20 minutes, basting periodically with sauce. Serve immediately.

LENTIL & QUINOA STUFFED POBLANOS

These large, mild peppers have a slightly smoky flavour when cooked and hold their shape well, making them perfect for this Tex-Mex stuffing.

MAKES 8 · PREP 20 MINS · COOK 30 MINS

4 poblano peppers (or green bell peppers)

1 tbsp olive oil

140g (5oz) cooked red quinoa

150g (5½oz) cooked beluga lentils

150g (5½oz) fresh sweetcorn kernels

1 tbsp ground cumin

1½ tsp chipotle chilli powder

¼ tsp chilli powder

½ tsp tomato purée

90ml (3fl oz) vegetable stock

15g (½oz) chopped coriander leaves

225g (8oz) soft goat's cheese

1 Preheat the oven to 190°C (375°F). Cut the peppers in half length-ways, leaving the stems intact, and remove the seeds. Drizzle with oil and arrange cut-side down in a 23 × 33cm (9 × 13in) glass baking dish. Roast for 10 minutes, or until tender, but still maintaining their shape.

2 Meanwhile, to make the stuffing, in a large mixing bowl combine the quinoa, lentils, corn, cumin, chipotle chilli powder, chilli powder, tomato purée, stock, coriander leaves, and half the goat's cheese.

3 To assemble, fill each roasted pepper half with an equal amount of the quinoa mixture and top with the remaining goat's cheese. Return to the oven and bake for 15 minutes until warmed through. Serve immediately.

Make it vegan

Replace the goat's cheese with a vegan cream cheese alternative.

Make it with meat

Add 125g (4½oz) cooked, chopped chicken to the quinoa mixture.

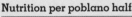

Nutrition per poblano half

Calories	290
Total Fat	11g
Saturated Fat	4.5g
Cholesterol	15mg
Sodium	150mg
Total Carbohydrate	38g
Dietary Fibre	7g
Sugars	1g
Protein	14g

Pulse exchange

Substitute an equal amount of **pinto beans** or **black beans** for the beluga lentils.

CHICKPEA FLOUR SOCCA
WITH HERB & GREEN OLIVE SALAD

Socca – a chickpea flour pancake – hails from the south of France. Its mild, nutty flavour is the perfect canvas for the fresh herbs and flavours of the rocket salad.

MAKES 2 · PREP 5 MINS, PLUS 1 HR FOR BATTER TO REST · COOK 15 MINS

100g (3½oz) chickpea flour

1 tsp smoked paprika

⅛ tsp garlic powder

pinch of salt

3 tbsp olive oil

240ml (8fl oz) water

45g (1½oz) rocket leaves

10g (¼oz) flat-leaf parsley

5g (⅛oz) basil leaves

45g (1½oz) pitted green olives, halved

juice of 1 lemon

1 To make the batter, in a medium mixing bowl add the chickpea flour, paprika, garlic powder, salt, 2 tablespoons oil, and water. Whisk to combine. Let rest at room temperature for 1 hour.

2 With the rack in the middle of the oven, place two 20cm (8in) cast-iron or ovenproof frying pans in the oven and preheat to 230°C (450°F). (The pans will heat up with the oven.)

3 When the frying pans are heated, carefully remove and swirl 1½ teaspoons oil around in each. Pour half the batter into each and return to the oven. Bake for 8 minutes. Then turn the grill onto a low setting and cook for an additional 2 minutes. Remove and let rest for 1–2 minutes.

4 Meanwhile, to make the herb and olive salad, toss together the rocket, parsley, basil, olives, and lemon juice. Place each socca on a serving plate and top with an equal amount of salad. Serve immediately.

Nutrition per socca

Calories	403
Total Fat	26g
Saturated Fat	3.5g
Cholesterol	0mg
Sodium	237mg
Total Carbohydrate	32g
Dietary Fibre	7g
Sugars	6g
Protein	12g

● **Make it with meat**

For a more filling meal, top the salad with sliced, grilled steak.

RED LENTIL LASAGNE

This classic Italian dish has all the rich creaminess of ricotta, mozzarella, and Parmesan, with the added protein and fibre of red lentils.

SERVES 12 · PREP 20 MINS · COOK 1 HR 30 MINS

1 tbsp olive oil

2 celery sticks, diced

2 small carrots, peeled and finely diced

1 onion, diced

2 garlic cloves, finely chopped

2 tsp chopped oregano

1 tsp chopped thyme

1 tsp chopped flat-leaf parsley

pinch of crushed dried chillies

500g (1lb 2oz) cooked red lentils

2 tbsp tomato purée

500g (16oz) passata

500g (16oz) chopped tomatoes

120ml (4fl oz) vegetable stock

salt and freshly ground black pepper

900g (2lb) ricotta cheese

1 large egg, beaten

300g (10oz) grated mozzarella cheese

2 tsp chopped basil

20g (¾oz) grated Parmesan cheese

250g (9oz) package oven-ready lasagne sheets

1 Preheat the oven to 180°C (350°F). In a large flameproof casserole, warm the oil over a medium-low heat. Add the celery, carrots, and onion and cook for 2–3 minutes until soft. Add the garlic and cook for an additional minute. Stir in the oregano, thyme, parsley, and crushed dried chillies.

2 Add the lentils, tomato purée, passata, chopped tomatoes, and stock. Bring to the boil then reduce to a simmer and cook for 20–25 minutes, until the lentils are tender. Season with salt and pepper to taste.

3 Meanwhile, in a large mixing bowl, stir together the ricotta, egg, 125g (4½oz) mozzarella, basil, and Parmesan.

4 To assemble, in a 23 × 33cm (9 × 13in) baking dish, lightly spread the lentil mixture to coat the bottom of the dish. Layer with 3 lasagne sheets, a third of the ricotta mixture, then a third of the lentil mixture. Repeat layers two more times for 3 layers total. Finally, top with 3 lasagne sheets, dot the top with any remaining lentil mixture, and sprinkle the remaining mozzarella over the top.

5 Cover the dish with foil and bake for 40 minutes. Remove the foil and cook for an additional 20 minutes. Leave to stand for 5–10 minutes before serving.

● **Make it with meat**

Cook 225g (8oz) minced turkey or beef along with the onion in step 1, before adding the garlic.

Nutrition per serving

Calories	290
Total Fat	14g
Saturated Fat	8g
Cholesterol	55mg
Sodium	250mg
Total Carbohydrate	27g
Dietary Fibre	5g
Sugars	6g
Protein	17g

Why not try ...

Sauté 100g (3½oz) baby spinach and layer on top of the ricotta as you assemble the lasagne.

BAKED FETA
IN TOMATO LENTIL SAUCE

A crowd-pleasing appetizer, this is also an easy dish to make. The hot, gooey feta and tangy, sweet tomato sauce will melt in your mouth – scoop up every last drop with the baguette slices.

SERVES 4 · PREP 15 MINS · COOK 50 MINS

1 tbsp olive oil

1 garlic clove, finely chopped

2 x 400g (14oz) cans chopped tomatoes

2 tsp chopped oregano

1 tbsp balsamic vinegar

pinch of crushed dried chillies

115g (4oz) cooked yellow lentils

salt and freshly ground black pepper

225g (8oz) feta cheese block

1 baguette, cut into 2.5cm (1in) slices, toasted

1 Heat the oven to 180°C (350°F). In a large saucepan, heat the oil over a medium-low heat until shimmering. Add the garlic and cook for 2–3 minutes until soft but not browned.

2 Incorporate the chopped tomatoes, oregano, vinegar, and crushed dried chillies. Bring to the boil and add the lentils. Simmer, covered, over a medium-low heat for 15 minutes, or until the tomato sauce is warmed through. Season with salt and pepper to taste.

3 Transfer the tomato sauce to a 3-litre (5-pint) casserole or baking dish. Cut the feta into 1cm (½in) slices and arrange in an even layer on top of the sauce.

4 Bake, uncovered, for 12 minutes, or until the feta is soft and slightly melted. Serve immediately with the baguette slices.

Nutrition per serving

Calories	330
Total Fat	16g
Saturated Fat	9g
Cholesterol	50mg
Sodium	950mg
Total Carbohydrate	34g
Dietary Fibre	8g
Sugars	12g
Protein	15g

Pulse exchange
Substitute an equal amount of **red lentils** for the yellow lentils.

BAKED LENTIL SPAGHETTI SQUASH
WITH WALNUTS & GOAT'S CHEESE

For infusing your diet with complex carbohydrates, spaghetti squash is a healthy alternative to pasta. Each squash half is its own nutty, casserole-type dish in a self-contained serving.

SERVES 2 · PREP 25 MINS · COOK 45 MINS

1 spaghetti squash

2 tbsp olive oil

450g (1lb) cooked green or Puy lentils

60g (2oz) walnuts, toasted and roughly chopped

1 tbsp thyme leaves

zest of 1 lemon

salt and freshly ground black pepper

115g (4oz) soft goat's cheese

1 Preheat the oven to 190°C (375°F). Cut the spaghetti squash in half lengthways and use a spoon to scrape the seeds out of each half. Drizzle each half with 1 tablespoon of oil, and arrange cut-side down on a baking tray. Cook for 30–35 minutes until tender but not mushy.

2 Meanwhile, in a medium mixing bowl, combine the lentils, walnuts, thyme, and lemon zest. Set aside until the squash is cooked.

3 With a fork, scrape the squash flesh to expose and fluff the spaghetti shreds. Season with salt and pepper. Divide the lentil filling evenly between the halves and crumble goat's cheese over each. Bake for an additional 10 minutes, or until the cheese softens. Serve immediately, directly from the squash shell.

Nutrition per serving

Calories	700
Total Fat	46g
Saturated Fat	12g
Cholesterol	25mg
Sodium	610mg
Total Carbohydrate	51g
Dietary Fibre	17g
Sugars	11g
Protein	30g

Pulse exchange

Use an equal amount of **mung beans** in place of the green or Puy lentils.

THREE BEAN PAELLA

This colourful twist on the classic Spanish dish features a trio of meaty pulses in addition to saffron-scented rice, roasted red peppers, and tangy green olives.

SERVES 10 · PREP 35 MINS · COOK 1 HR 5 MINS

2 tbsp olive oil

1 onion, chopped

3 garlic cloves, finely chopped

pinch of saffron threads

pinch of crushed dried chillies

225g (8oz) chopped tomatoes

1 tsp smoked paprika

450g (1lb) uncooked paella rice, such as Bomba or Calisparra

750ml (1¼ pints) vegetable stock

175g (6oz) cooked haricot beans

115g (4oz) cooked pigeon peas, or black-eyed beans

125g (4½oz) cooked kidney beans

60g (2oz) frozen green peas, thawed

60g (2oz) roasted red pepper strips

60g (2oz) pitted, sliced green Spanish olives

1 large lemon, cut into 8 wedges

flat-leaf parsley, to garnish

1 In a 25cm (10in) paella pan or large cast-iron frying pan, warm the oil over a medium heat until shimmering. Add the onion and cook for 2 minutes, or until it starts to soften. Stir in the garlic and cook for 30 seconds, or until fragrant. Incorporate the saffron, dried chillies, tomatoes, and paprika. Stir in the rice and cook for 2–3 minutes.

2 Add the stock to the rice mixture and stir. Bring to the boil then reduce the heat to low and cook, covered, for 20 minutes. Stir in the haricot beans, pigeon peas (or black-eyed beans), and kidney beans. Cover again and cook for an additional 10 minutes. Scatter the green peas across the top and cook without stirring, covered, for another 10 minutes, or until the beans and peas are warmed through. Remove from the heat.

3 Season with salt and pepper to taste. Arrange the red pepper strips and olives evenly across the top. Cover and let the paella stand for 5 minutes. Garnish with lemon wedges and parsley, then serve.

Nutrition per serving

Calories	290
Total Fat	4.5g
Saturated Fat	0.5g
Cholesterol	0mg
Sodium	260mg
Total Carbohydrate	55g
Dietary Fibre	6g
Sugars	4g
Protein	8g

● **Make it with meat**

Add 225g (8oz) cooked, peeled, and de-veined prawns along with the red pepper strips in step 3.

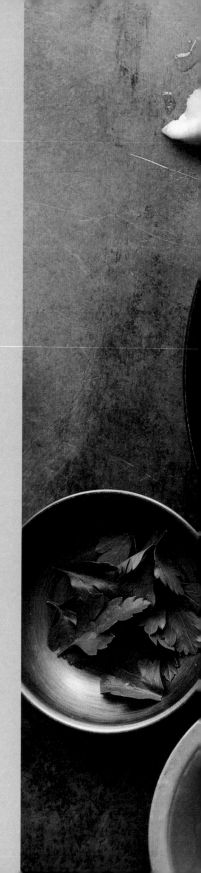

BUTTER BEAN ENCHILADAS

Tomatillos are a staple in Mexican sauces. Their tart, fruity flavour shines in this herby enchilada sauce, wonderfully set off by buttery beans and a sweet medley of vegetables.

● **Make it with meat**
Omit one courgette and add 125g (4½oz) cooked, chopped chicken or pork to the filling.

MAKES 10 · PREP 55 MINS · COOK 1 HR

- 675g (1½lb) tomatillos, husks removed, roughly chopped (or small, unripe tomatoes, roughly chopped)
- 2 medium jalapeños, deseeded and chopped
- 1 onion, chopped
- 30g (1oz) sprigs of coriander
- 175ml (6fl oz) vegetable stock
- salt and freshly ground black pepper
- 1 tbsp vegetable oil
- 1 garlic clove, finely chopped
- 2 courgettes, diced
- 150g (5½oz) fresh sweetcorn kernels
- 175g (6oz) baby spinach
- 1½ tsp ground cumin
- 1 tsp ground coriander
- pinch of crushed dried chillies
- 225g (8oz) cooked butter beans
- 10 small corn tortillas
- 225g (8oz) grated Monterey Jack or mozzarella cheese
- 15g (½oz) chopped coriander leaves

1 Preheat the oven to 180°C (350°F). On a lightly oiled baking tray, arrange the tomatillos, jalapeños, and onion. Roast for 20–25 minutes until tender. Leave to cool slightly. To make the sauce, transfer the roasted vegetables to a blender and combine with the coriander sprigs and stock. Blend until completely smooth. Season with salt and pepper.

2 To make the filling, in a large frying pan heat the oil over a medium-low heat. Add the garlic and cook for 1–2 minutes until soft. Add the courgettes and sweetcorn and cook, covered, for an additional 2–3 minutes until the courgette starts to become tender. Stir in the spinach, cumin, coriander, and dried chillies. Cover and cook for another 3–4 minutes until the spinach wilts slightly. Stir in the butter beans. Season with salt and pepper to taste. Remove from the heat and leave to cool slightly.

3 Lightly oil a 23 × 30cm (9 × 12in) glass or ceramic baking dish. Lightly coat the bottom with sauce. To assemble, work with one tortilla at a time on a clean, flat work surface. Place 4 tablespoons of filling onto the tortilla and top with 1½–2 tablespoons of greated cheese. Roll tightly and place seam-side down in the dish. Repeat to make 10 enchiladas in total.

4 Top the enchiladas with the remaining sauce. Sprinkle the remaining cheese over the top. Cover with foil and bake for 15 minutes. Uncover and bake for another 10 minutes, or until the cheese melts. Garnish with chopped coriander and serve immediately.

Nutrition per enchilada

Calories	180
Total Fat	6g
Saturated Fat	3g
Cholesterol	10mg
Sodium	340mg
Total Carbohydrate	23g
Dietary Fibre	5g
Sugars	5g
Protein	10g

Why not try...
Use crumbled feta instead of grated cheese. Place 1 tablespoon inside each enchildada and sprinkle the rest on top.

MEXICAN TAMALE SKILLET PIE

Tamales are a traditional Mexican dish made from masa (corn) filled with meat or vegetables. Here, the tamale is a cornbread topping for spicy beans.

SERVES 10 · PREP 40 MINS · COOK 45 MINS

● **Make it with meat**

Brown 225g (8oz) raw minced beef or turkey along with the garlic.

1 tbsp olive oil

1 onion, diced

1 garlic clove, finely chopped

1 small jalapeño, deseeded and minced

1 red pepper, deseeded and diced

1 courgette, diced

sweetcorn kernels from 3 cobs, about 225g (8oz)

1 tsp chipotle chilli powder

1 tbsp ground cumin

400g (14oz) can chopped tomatoes

2 tbsp tomato purée

180ml (6fl oz) vegetable stock

225g (8oz) cooked pinto beans

175g (6oz) cooked kidney beans

100g (3½oz) plain flour

115g (4oz) yellow polenta (cornmeal)

1 tsp salt

1 tsp sugar

¾ tsp baking powder

¼ tsp bicarbonate of soda

180ml (6fl oz) full-fat milk

1 large egg

3 tbsp unsalted butter, melted

1 Preheat the oven to 220°C (425°F). In a 25cm (10in) cast-iron or ovenproof frying pan, warm the oil over medium heat. Add the onion and cook for 2–3 minutes until soft. Add the garlic and jalapeño and cook for an additional minute.

2 Add the pepper, courgette, and sweetcorn. Cook for 2–3 minutes. Add the chipotle chilli powder and cumin. Pour in the chopped tomatoes, tomato purée, stock, pinto beans, and kidney beans. Mix thoroughly. Bring to the boil then reduce to a simmer over a low heat and cook for 8–10 minutes. Remove from the heat.

3 Meanwhile, in a large mixing bowl whisk together the flour, polenta, salt, sugar, baking powder, and bicarbonate of soda.

4 In a small bowl, mix together the milk and egg. To make the cornbread, add the milk-egg mixture to the flour mixture. Then drizzle in the melted butter and stir.

5 To assemble, spread the cornbread mixture across the top. Bake for 15 minutes, or until the cornbread is completely baked and light golden brown. Serve immediately.

Nutrition per serving

Calories	280
Total Fat	8g
Saturated Fat	3g
Cholesterol	30mg
Sodium	170mg
Total Carbohydrate	45g
Dietary Fibre	6g
Sugars	5g
Protein	7g

Pulse exchange

Substitute 325g (11oz) cooked **pigeon peas** for the kidney beans.

PIGEON PEA SAMOSA BAKE

Filled with the unique aromas and flavours of Indian spiced potatoes and pigeon peas, this casserole with its crunchy filo topping is a nod to traditional samosa pastry.

SERVES 8 · PREP 30 MINS · COOK 45 MINS

550g (1¼lb) peeled and diced potatoes

115g (4oz) frozen green peas, thawed

3 tbsp ghee

1 small onion, diced

1 small green chilli, deseeded and finely chopped

¼ tsp ground ginger

¼ tsp ground coriander

¾ tsp garam masala

1 tsp ground cumin

¼ tsp turmeric

¼ tsp ground cayenne pepper

¾ tsp curry powder

1 tbsp water

75g (2½oz) cooked pigeon peas, or black-eyed beans

90ml (3fl oz) vegetable stock

10g (¼oz) chopped coriander leaves

4 sheets of frozen filo pastry, thawed

Nutrition per serving

Calories	150
Total Fat	4.5g
Saturated Fat	2.5g
Cholesterol	5mg
Sodium	75mg
Total Carbohydrate	25g
Dietary Fibre	3g
Sugars	2g
Protein	4g

1 Preheat the oven to 180°C (350°F). Lightly oil a 23cm (9in) round baking dish.

2 Bring a large saucepan of water to a rapid boil. Add the potatoes and cook for 8–10 minutes until tender to the point of a knife. Meanwhile, place the green peas in a sieve or colander. When the potatoes are cooked, pour the potatoes and hot water over the peas. Let drain thoroughly.

3 In a 30cm (12in) frying pan, heat 2 tablespoons of ghee over a medium-low heat until shimmering. Add the onion and chilli and cook for 2–3 minutes until soft. Incorporate the ginger, ground coriander, garam masala, cumin, turmeric, cayenne, curry powder, and water. Cook for an additional minute until the spices are warmed through.

4 Add the potatoes and green peas, pigeon peas (or black-eyed beans), stock, chopped coriander, and remaining 1 tablespoon ghee. Stir to combine. Season with salt and pepper to taste. Remove from the heat.

5 Transfer the mixture to the baking dish. Crinkle the filo sheet and place atop the potato mixture. Bake for 20–25 minutes until the filo pastry is golden brown, then serve.

● **Make it vegan**

Replace the ghee with vegetable or rapeseed oil.

● **Make it with meat**

Add 125g (4½oz) cooked, seasoned minced lamb with the peas in step 4.

Why not try...
For an aromatic garnish, sprinkle the pastry with crushed cumin seeds before baking.

BLACK-EYED BEAN CHILAQUILES

This traditional Mexican dish is an excellent way to use leftover tortillas. Baked with black-eyed beans and a spicy tomato sauce, they are transformed into savoury breakfast food.

SERVES 4 · PREP 20 MINS · COOK 45 MINS

8 small corn tortillas, cut into sixths

3 tbsp vegetable oil

2 garlic cloves, finely chopped

1½ tsp dried oregano

3 tsp ancho chilli powder

1½ tsp ground cumin

½ tsp ground cayenne pepper

400g (14oz) can tomato sauce or passata

240ml (8fl oz) water

175g (6oz) cooked black-eyed beans

175g (6oz) crumbled feta cheese

3 spring onions, chopped

1 small jalapeño, thinly sliced

30g (1oz) coriander leaves

1 Preheat the oven to 170°C (325°F). To make the tortilla chips, toss the cut tortilla pieces in 2 tablespoons oil. Arrange on a baking sheet and bake for 15–20 minutes until crisp and golden brown.

2 Meanwhile, to make the sauce, in a saucepan heat the remaining 1 tablespoon oil over a medium-low heat. Add the garlic and cook for 1–2 minutes until soft but not brown. Stir in the oregano, ancho chilli powder, cumin, cayenne, tomato sauce or passata, and water. Bring to the boil then reduce the heat and simmer for 15 minutes, or until slightly thickened.

3 In a large mixing bowl, toss the tortilla chips with the black-eyed beans and about two-thirds of the sauce. Arrange in a baking dish. Sprinkle the feta on top. Bake for 8–10 minutes until the cheese is melted.

4 Garnish with the spring onion, jalapeño, and coriander leaves. Serve immediately with the remaining sauce on the side.

● **Make it with meat**

Layer 125g (4½oz) cooked, chopped chicken or pork before adding the cheese in step 3.

Nutrition per serving

Calories	380
Total Fat	18g
Saturated Fat	11g
Cholesterol	45mg
Sodium	750mg
Total Carbohydrate	41g
Dietary Fibre	7g
Sugars	6g
Protein	15g

Why not try...
Top with one runny, fried egg per portion and serve for brunch.

GREEK AUBERGINE & LENTIL BAKE

This three-cheese casserole, inspired by Greek moussaka, combines lentils and aubergine for a robust main course.

SERVES 8 · PREP 45 MINS · COOK 1 HR 15 MINS

● **Make it with meat**

Reduce the lentils by half and stir in 350g (12oz) cooked minced lamb or beef in step 4.

1 aubergine, about 225g (8oz)

3–4 tbsp olive oil

1 small onion, finely diced

1 orange or yellow pepper, deseeded and diced

1 garlic clove, finely chopped

2 tbsp tomato purée

400g (14oz) cooked green or Puy lentils

350g (12oz) passata

¼ tsp ground nutmeg

1 tsp cinnamon

salt and freshly ground black pepper

225g (8oz) ricotta cheese

250g (9oz) plain Greek-style yogurt

60g (2oz) crumbled feta cheese

1 large egg

3 tbsp finely grated Parmesan cheese

2 tbsp chopped flat-leaf parsley, to garnish

1 Preheat the oven to 180°C (375°F). Lightly oil a 2.5-litre (4½-pint) baking dish. Slice the aubergine into 1cm (½in) thick rounds.

2 In a large non-stick frying pan, heat ½ tablespoon of oil over a medium heat until shimmering. Working in batches, cook the aubergine slices for 2–3 minutes per side until tender and light golden brown, adding an additional ½ tablespoon oil to the frying pan when turning. Remove the slices from the frying pan and place on a plate lined with kitchen paper to absorb oil.

3 In the same frying pan, heat the remaining 1 tablespoon oil over a medium-low heat until warm. Add the onion and diced pepper and cook for 2–3 minutes until soft. Add the garlic and cook for an additional minute.

4 Add the tomato purée, lentils, passata, nutmeg, and cinnamon. Stir to combine. Season with salt and pepper to taste and remove from the heat.

5 Line the baking dish with a single layer of aubergine slices. Spread the lentil mixture on top. Cover with another layer of aubergine slices.

6 In a large mixing bowl, whisk together the ricotta, yogurt, feta, and egg. Spread the mixture evenly over the aubergine. Sprinkle the Parmesan over the top.

7 Bake for 30–35 minutes, uncovered, until the top is set and golden brown. Garnish with parsley and leave to rest for 15 minutes before serving.

Nutrition per serving

Calories	240
Total Fat	13g
Saturated Fat	5g
Cholesterol	50mg
Sodium	430mg
Total Carbohydrate	19g
Dietary Fibre	6g
Sugars	7g
Protein	13g

SPICED SWEET POTATO SHEPHERD'S PIE

Sweet potato works wonderfully with the warm spices in this Indian-inspired twist on a classic comfort dish.

SERVES 6 · PREP 35 MINS · COOK 50 MINS

3 sweet potatoes

75ml (2½fl oz) double cream

salt and freshly ground black pepper

2 tbsp ghee

1 onion, chopped

1 garlic clove, finely chopped

500g (1lb 2oz) cooked brown lentils

1 tbsp ground cumin

1 tbsp garam masala

2 tsp curry powder

1 tsp turmeric

400ml (14fl oz) vegetable stock

15g (½oz) chopped coriander leaves

45g (1½oz) panko breadcrumbs

1 Preheat the oven to 190°C (375°F). Peel and dice the sweet potatoes. In a large saucepan, bring 1.5 litres (2½ pints) water to the boil. Cook the potatoes for 15–20 minutes until tender to the point of a knife. Drain thoroughly and transfer to a large mixing bowl. With a potato masher, mash the potatoes and double cream until smooth. Season with salt and pepper to taste.

2 Meanwhile, in a large frying pan warm the ghee over a medium heat. Add the onion and cook for 2 minutes, or until soft. Add the garlic and cook for an additional minute.

3 Add the lentils, cumin, garam masala, curry powder, and turmeric. Stir to combine and cook for 1–2 minutes to warm the spices. Add the stock and cook for 5 minutes. Stir in the chopped coriander.

4 Pour the lentil mixture evenly into a 23 × 30cm (9 x 12in) glass or ceramic baking dish. Top with the mashed sweet potato. Bake for 15 minutes. Sprinkle evenly with the breadcrumbs and bake for another 10 minutes, or until lightly browned. Cool for 10 minutes before serving.

● Make it vegan

Substitute a vegan butter alternative or rapeseed oil for the ghee.

● Make it with meat

Reduce the lentils by half. Brown 450g (1lb) raw minced lamb, along with the onions.

Nutrition per serving

Calories	310
Total Fat	8g
Saturated Fat	4g
Cholesterol	20mg
Sodium	90mg
Total Carbohydrate	47g
Dietary Fibre	13g
Sugars	7g
Protein	14g

Pulse exchange

Instead of brown lentils, use an equal amount of cooked **green lentils.**

KIDNEY BEAN CASSOULET

The flaky breadcrumb topping contrasts with the buttery kidney beans in this hearty, filling main course.

SERVES 4 · PREP 20 MINS · COOK 1 HR

2 tbsp olive oil

1 small onion, diced

1 carrot, diced

1 celery stick, diced

2 garlic cloves, finely chopped

3 sprigs of thyme

1 bay leaf

pinch of crushed dried chillies

300g (10oz) cooked kidney beans

175g (6oz) passata

180ml (6fl oz) vegetable stock

salt and freshly ground black pepper

50g (1¾oz) panko breadcrumbs

1 tbsp chopped flat-leaf parsley

1 Preheat the oven to 200°C (400°F). Lightly oil a 2-litre (3½-pint) baking dish.

2 In a stock pot or flameproof casserole, heat the oil over a medium-low heat. Add the onion, carrot, and celery, and cook for 2–3 minutes until soft. Add the garlic and cook for an additional minute.

3 Incorporate the thyme, bay leaf, chillies, kidney beans, passata, and stock. Simmer, covered, for 20 minutes.

4 Remove the bay leaf and thyme stems. In a blender or food processor, purée about 120ml (4fl oz) of the bean mixture until smooth. Return the puréed mixture to the pot and stir to combine. Season with salt and pepper to taste. Transfer the bean mixture to the baking dish.

5 To make the topping, in a small bowl combine the breadcrumbs and parsley. Top the dish evenly with the breadcrumb mixture. Bake for 20 minutes, or until golden brown. Serve immediately.

Nutrition per serving

Calories	330
Total Fat	8g
Saturated Fat	1g
Cholesterol	0mg
Sodium	95mg
Total Carbohydrate	51g
Dietary Fibre	14g
Sugars	5g
Protein	16g

● **Make it with meat**

Incorporate 125g (4½oz) cooked, chopped pork or duck, just before transferring to the baking dish in step 4.

BROWN LENTIL & MUSHROOM POT PIE

Lentils and mushrooms covered in flaky puff pastry make for a cosy, comforting winter meal.

SERVES 4 · PREP 25 MINS · COOK 45 MINS

1 tbsp olive oil

1 celery stick, diced

1 small onion, diced

2 carrots, diced

1 garlic clove, finely chopped

1 tsp chopped rosemary

3 sprigs of thyme

225g (8oz) cremini or button mushrooms, quartered

240ml (8fl oz) vegetable stock

2 tbsp tomato purée

2 tsp soy sauce

2 tsp cornflour

2 tsp cold water

250g (9oz) cooked brown lentils

salt and freshly ground black pepper

1 sheet puff pastry, ½ of a 500g (1lb) package

1 Preheat the oven to 200°C (400°F). Lightly oil a 1-litre (2-pint) baking dish. In a large frying pan, heat the oil over a medium-low heat. Add the celery, onion, and carrot. Cook for 2–3 minutes until soft. Add the garlic and cook for 1–2 minutes.

2 Increase the heat to medium and add the rosemary, thyme, and mushrooms. Cook for an additional 4–5 minutes until the mushrooms reduce in size and caramelize. Pour in the stock, tomato purée, and soy sauce. Bring to the boil then reduce the heat and simmer, covered, for 5–10 minutes until heated through.

3 In a small bowl, whisk together the cornflour and water. Stir into the mushroom mixture, bring to the boil, then reduce the heat to low. Add the lentils and stir to combine thoroughly. Cook, covered, for 5 minutes, or until thickened. Season with salt and pepper to taste. Remove the thyme stems.

4 Transfer the lentil mixture to the baking dish. Cover with the puff pastry sheet, rolling first if necessary to make it fit. Trim the sides to leave a 3cm (1in) overhang all around. Bake for 25 minutes, or until the pastry is cooked and golden brown. Let sit for 5 minutes before serving.

Make it vegan

Replace the soy sauce with an equal amount of liquid aminos.

Make it with meat

To add umami flavour, use the same amount of beef stock instead of vegetable stock – taste before adding any additional salt.

Pulse exchange

Instead of brown lentils, use 650g (1lb 2oz) cooked **green** or **Puy lentils.**

Nutrition per serving

Calories	440
Total Fat	20g
Saturated Fat	4g
Cholesterol	0mg
Sodium	350mg
Total Carbohydrate	50g
Dietary Fibre	11g
Sugars	7g
Protein	15g

SWEET POTATO & ADZUKI BEAN GRATIN

A golden breadcrumb crust tops this hearty gratin, flavoured with sage and onion. Serve with bread and salad for a perfect autumn meal.

SERVES 6 · PREP 30 MINS · COOK 40 MINS

2 tbsp vegetable oil

1 large sweet potato, peeled and diced

1 small onion, diced

1 carrot, diced

1 garlic clove, finely chopped

pinch of crushed dried chillies

¾ tsp chopped sage

1 tsp soy sauce

240ml (8fl oz) vegetable stock

325g (11oz) cooked adzuki beans

60g (2oz) panko breadcrumbs

2 tbsp grated Parmesan cheese

flat-leaf parsley, to garnish

1 Preheat the oven to 190°C (375°F). Toss 1 tablespoon oil with the sweet potato cubes. Arrange on a baking tray and roast for 20 minutes, or until tender and lightly caramelized. Let cool slightly. Keep the oven heated.

2 In a large frying pan, heat the remaining 1 tablespoon oil over a medium-low heat. Add the onion and carrot and cook for 2–3 minutes until soft. Add the garlic and cook for another 1–2 minutes.

3 Stir in the crushed dried chillies, sage, soy sauce, stock, and adzuki beans. Add the sweet potato. Cook over a medium-low heat for 5 minutes, or until the ingredients are heated through and the liquid reduces.

4 To make the topping, in a small bowl combine the breadcrumbs and Parmesan. Set aside.

5 Transfer the sweet potato mixture to a 1-litre (2-pint) glass baking dish. Top evenly with the breadcrumb mixture. Bake, uncovered, for 20–25 minutes until crisp and golden brown. Let sit for 5 minutes, then garnish with parsley and serve.

Nutrition per serving

Calories	180
Total Fat	5g
Saturated Fat	4g
Cholesterol	0mg
Sodium	140mg
Total Carbohydrate	27g
Dietary Fibre	6g
Sugars	4g
Protein	6g

Why not try... For a fried sage garnish, in a shallow frying pan, heat 1 tablespoon olive oil and fry 4–5 whole sage leaves for 10–15 seconds each.

DESSERTS

FLOURLESS BLACK BEAN BROWNIES

These brownies are not like other flourless bakes you've tried – they're light, moist, and cakey.

MAKES 12 · PREP 15 MINS · COOK 1 HR

350g (12oz) cooked black
  beans

120ml (4fl oz) agave nectar

60g (2oz) coconut oil

1 tsp vanilla extract

zest of 1 orange

¼ tsp salt

½ tsp baking powder

75g (2½oz) sugar

45g (1½oz) unsweetened
  cocoa powder

3 large eggs, beaten

85g (3oz) dark chocolate chips

1 Preheat the oven to 180°C (350°F). Lightly oil a 28 x 18cm (11 x 7in) metal baking tin. In a food processor, combine the black beans, agave, coconut oil, vanilla extract, and orange zest until smooth.

2 In a large mixing bowl, combine the salt, baking powder, sugar, and cocoa powder. Incorporate the black bean mixture and eggs.

3 Gently fold in the chocolate chips, being careful not to overwork the mixture.

4 Pour the mixture into the baking tin. Bake for 30–35 minutes, until the brownies pull away from the edge and a skewer inserted into the centre comes out clean. Leave to cool for 15–20 minutes before cutting and serving.

Nutrition per brownie

Calories	170
Total Fat	10g
Saturated Fat	7g
Cholesterol	45mg
Sodium	65mg
Total Carbohydrate	18g
Dietary Fibre	5g
Sugars	7g
Protein	5g

● **Make it vegan**

Replace the eggs with 225g (8oz) unsweetened apple sauce or purée.

COCONUT WHITE BEAN TRES LECHES CAKE

Tres leches cake is a traditional Mexican dessert, which is soaked in three kinds of milk. Here, coconut milk adds a flavourful twist to the classic recipe.

SERVES 16 · PREP 30 MINS · COOK 30 MINS, PLUS 2 HRS 15 MINS TO COOL & CHILL

½ tsp baking powder

75g (2½oz) wholemeal plain flour

75g (2½oz) white bean flour

pinch of salt

5 large eggs, whites and yolks separated

200g (7oz) sugar

80ml (2½fl oz) unsweetened almond milk

1 tsp vanilla extract

350ml (12fl oz) evaporated milk

400g (14oz) can sweetened condensed milk

165ml (5½fl oz) coconut milk

350ml (12fl oz) double cream

60g (2oz) unsweetened, shredded coconut flakes, toasted

1 Preheat the oven to 180°C (350°F). Oil a 23 x 30cm (9 x 12in) glass baking dish. In a large mixing bowl, combine the baking powder, wholemeal flour, white bean flour, and salt.

2 In a large mixing bowl, with the whisk attachment of an electric mixer, beat the egg yolks and 150g (5½oz) sugar for 2–3 minutes until a very pale, light yellow. Stir in the almond milk and vanilla. Add the egg mixture to the flour mixture and stir to incorporate.

3 Clean the egg mixing bowl and add the egg whites and remaining 50g (1½oz) sugar. Beat the whites on a medium speed for 4–5 minutes until stiff peaks form. Gently fold the egg whites into the egg-flour mixture.

4 Transfer the mixture to the baking dish, spreading evenly, and bake for 35–40 minutes, until a skewer inserted into the centre comes out clean. Leave to cool for 30 minutes.

5 Meanwhile, in a small saucepan, combine the evaporated milk, condensed milk, and coconut milk. Bring to the boil, stirring occasionally, then remove from the heat and leave to cool completely.

6 With a fork or wooden skewer, generously poke holes through the cake. Evenly pour the milk mixture over the cake (you may not need the entire amount; the milk should fill the dish about halfway). Cover with foil and refrigerate for 45 minutes, letting the cake absorb the milk.

7 Once the cake has rested, in a small bowl whip the double cream until soft peaks form. Spread the cream evenly over the top of the cake then sprinkle with the toasted coconut. Refrigerate once more for 1 hour or overnight. Store tightly covered in the fridge for up to 2 days.

Nutrition per serving

Calories	360
Total Fat	19g
Saturated Fat	12g
Cholesterol	105mg
Sodium	140mg
Total Carbohydrate	41g
Dietary Fibre	2g
Sugars	34g
Protein	8g

COCONUT & BEAN ICE CREAM

Home-made red bean paste makes this less cloyingly sweet than a commercial ice cream.

SERVES 8 · PREP 25 MINS, PLUS 2 HRS TO FREEZE

400g (14oz) cooked adzuki
   beans
125g (4½oz) light brown
   sugar
100g (3½oz) granulated
   sugar
350ml (12fl oz) double
   cream

350ml (12fl oz) full-fat
   milk
pinch of salt
75g (2½oz) sweetened,
   coconut flakes, toasted

1 To make the paste, in a food processor combine the adzuki beans and brown sugar. Pulse until smooth. Transfer to a large mixing bowl.

2 In the mixing bowl, whisk in the granulated sugar, double cream, milk, and salt.

3 In the frozen bowl of an electric ice cream maker, add the cream mixture and churn for 15–20 minutes until the texture of soft serve ice cream. Add the coconut and churn for an additional minute, or until completely combined.

4 Remove the ice cream mixture from the frozen bowl and transfer to an airtight, freezer safe storage container. Freeze for 2 hours or overnight before serving.

Nutrition per serving

Calories	400
Total Fat	20g
Saturated Fat	13g
Cholesterol	65mg
Sodium	135mg
Total Carbohydrate	52g
Dietary Fibre	5g
Sugars	37g
Protein	7g

● **Make it vegan**

Replace the double cream with coconut cream and replace the milk with coconut milk.

ADZUKI BEAN & CHERRY POPS

The tartness of cherries is a wonderful match for the creaminess of the coconut milk and adzuki beans in this frozen treat.

MAKES 10 · PREP 15 MINS, PLUS 6 HRS TO FREEZE

350g (12oz) frozen pitted
   dark, sweet cherries
100g (3½oz) cooked
   adzuki beans

400ml (14fl oz) can
   coconut milk
3 tsp sugar

1 Slightly thaw then roughly chop about 50g (1¾oz) cherries and set aside. In a blender, combine the adzuki beans, coconut milk, sugar, and remaining cherries. Purée until completely smooth. Strain the mixture through a fine sieve to remove the tough skins.

2 Place approximately ¼ teaspoon chopped cherries in the bottom of each lollipop mould to make 10 lollies in total. Pour an equal amount of the blended adzuki bean mixture into the moulds. Insert a lolly stick into each. Freeze for 6 hours or overnight.

Nutrition per lollipop

Calories	100
Total Fat	7g
Saturated Fat	6g
Cholesterol	0mg
Sodium	10mg
Total Carbohydrate	9g
Dietary Fibre	1g
Sugars	5g
Protein	2g

LENTIL BAKLAVA

There's nothing like baklava – a sticky, rich treat of flaky filo pastry, nuts, and honey. Brown lentils add nutritional value to this decadent dessert.

● **Make it vegan**

Use agave nectar rather than honey and replace the butter with a vegan alternative.

MAKES 24 · PREP 1 HR · COOK 1 HR

200g (7oz) sugar

80ml (2½fl oz) honey

180ml (6fl oz) water

3 sprigs of thyme

juice and peel of 1 large orange

225g (8oz) chopped pistachios

225g (8oz) chopped walnuts

250g (9oz) cooked brown lentils

1½ tsp cinnamon

¾ tsp ground cardamom

pinch of salt

12 tbsp unsalted butter, melted

450g (1lb) package frozen filo dough, thawed

1 To make the syrup, in a small saucepan combine 50g (1½oz) sugar, the honey, and water. Bring to the boil and boil gently, stirring occasionally, until the sugar dissolves. Add the thyme and orange juice and peel. Cook over a medium-low heat for 10 minutes until slightly thickened. Remove the peel and thyme stems. Remove from heat and leave to cool.

2 Meanwhile, in a large bowl, combine the pistachios, walnuts, lentils, cinnamon, cardamom, remaining 150g (5½oz) sugar, and salt.

3 Preheat the oven to 175°C (350°F). Prepare a clean, flat work space. Brush the bottom and sides of a 23 x 30cm (9 x 12in) metal baking tin with melted butter. Trim the filo dough to fit the tin and cover with a damp cloth to prevent it drying as you work.

4 Place 8 filo sheets into the bottom of the tin, brushing every other layer with butter. Spread about ⅓ of the nut mixture on top of the pastry and distribute evenly. Repeat this process 2 more times to form 3 nut layers in total.

5 Top the pastry with 8 more sheets of filo dough, and generously brush the top layer with melted butter. Score through the layers of pastry about three-quarters of the way down with a sharp knife, leaving the bottom intact, making 24 square or diamond-shaped pieces.

6 Bake for 40–45 minutes until golden brown. Leave to cool for 5 minutes. Cut through the scored lines to the bottom of the tin. Spoon the cooled syrup over the lines. Let cool completely. Refrigerate, covered, for at least 3 hours or overnight before serving. Store up to 3 days in an airtight container in the fridge.

Nutrition per piece

Calories	260
Total Fat	16g
Saturated Fat	6g
Cholesterol	20mg
Sodium	125mg
Total Carbohydrate	26g
Dietary Fibre	3g
Sugars	13g
Protein	5g

ADZUKI BEAN CHOCOLATE PUDDING

A little goes a long way – this chocolate pudding is rich, smooth, and decadent, with a nutty flavour. Serve it with a raspberry garnish.

SERVES 6 · PREP 10 MINS, PLUS OVERNIGHT TO SET · COOK 20 MINS

3 tbsp cornflour

2 tbsp plus 80ml (2¾fl oz) water

200g (7oz) cooked adzuki beans

240ml (8fl oz) unsweetened almond milk

2 tsp vanilla bean paste

60ml (2fl oz) agave nectar

45g (1½oz) unsweetened cocoa powder

6 raspberries, to garnish

1 In a small bowl, whisk together the cornflour and 2 tablespoons of water. Set aside.

2 In a blender, purée the adzuki beans with the remaining water and 120ml (4fl oz) almond milk until smooth.

3 In a small saucepan, whisk together the remaining 120ml (4fl oz) almond milk, vanilla bean paste, agave, cocoa powder, and puréed adzuki beans until completely smooth.

4 Heat the almond milk mixture over a low heat for 8–10 minutes until the mixture reaches a low simmer, stirring occasionally to avoid lumps. Remove from the heat and let sit at room temperature for 10 minutes.

5 Divide evenly among 6 serving cups, cover, and refrigerate overnight to set. Top each with a raspberry before serving.

Nutrition per serving

Calories	110
Total Fat	1.5g
Saturated Fat	0.5g
Cholesterol	0mg
Sodium	35mg
Total Carbohydrate	24g
Dietary Fibre	5g
Sugars	10g
Protein	4g

Pulse exchange

Instead of adzuki beans, use 125g (4½oz) cooked **black beans**.

STRAWBERRY & GREEN LENTIL CRISP

The natural sweetness of the strawberries pairs brilliantly with the caramelized topping in this dessert. It's a great way to use leftover fruit – you can substitute any you have on hand.

SERVES 6 · PREP 30 MINS · COOK 1 HR 10 MINS

150g (5½oz) cooked green lentils

675g (1½lb) strawberries, hulled and quartered

2 tbsp light brown sugar

3 tsp vanilla extract

1 tbsp cornflour

115g (4oz) wholemeal flour

75g (2½oz) coarsely chopped almonds

30g (1oz) rolled oats

75g (2½oz) sugar

1½ tsp cinnamon

115g (4oz) unsalted butter, melted

1 Preheat the oven to 180°C (350°F). Spread the lentils in an even layer on a baking tray. Toast for 20 minutes, or until dry and crispy.

2 In a 20 x 20cm (8 x 8in) glass baking dish, combine the strawberries, brown sugar, vanilla, and cornflour. Spread in an even layer.

3 To make the crisp topping, in a large mixing bowl combine the lentils, wholemeal flour, almonds, oats, sugar, and cinnamon. Drizzle in the melted butter and gently combine. Dollop the topping across the top of the strawberry mixture.

4 Bake, uncovered, for 40 minutes, or until the strawberry mixture bubbles and the topping browns. Let cool for 15–20 minutes before serving.

● Make it vegan

Replace the butter with a dairy-free butter alternative.

Pulse exchange

Use an equal amount of cooked **moth beans** or **black lentils** instead of the green lentils.

Nutrition per serving

Calories	450
Total Fat	23g
Saturated Fat	10g
Cholesterol	40mg
Sodium	0mg
Total Carbohydrate	54g
Dietary Fibre	9g
Sugars	25g
Protein	9g

WHITE BEAN CRÊPES
WITH APRICOT SAUCE

Crêpes are an easy dessert that's sure to impress. A tart apricot sauce makes a superb contrast for these nutty white bean crêpes.

MAKES 12 · PREP 30 MINS · COOK 50 MINS

225g (8oz) fresh apricots, pitted and roughly chopped

2 tbsp plus 2 tsp honey

juice of 1 orange

½ tsp vanilla bean paste

½ tbsp orange marmalade

60ml (2fl oz) water

140g (5oz) white bean flour

2½ tbsp sugar

1 tsp cinnamon

2 tbsp vegetable oil

120ml (4fl oz) water

240ml (8fl oz) unsweetened almond milk

2 tbsp vanilla extract

2 large eggs

zest of 1 large orange

60g (2oz) chopped, toasted hazelnuts

toasted desiccated coconut, to garnish

1 To make the apricot sauce, in a medium saucepan combine the apricots, honey, orange juice, vanilla bean paste, marmalade, and water. Bring to the boil then reduce the heat and simmer, covered, for 20 minutes, stirring occasionally. Let cool then transfer to a blender and purée until smooth. Set aside.

2 To make the crêpe batter, in a large mixing bowl combine the white bean flour, sugar, and cinnamon. In a medium mixing bowl, whisk together the oil, water, almond milk, vanilla extract, eggs, and orange zest. Pour the almond milk mixture into the flour mixture and stir until completely combined and smooth.

3 Heat a crêpe pan or a 15cm (6in) non-stick frying pan over a medium heat. Pour in 4 tablespoons batter and gently swirl around the bottom of the pan. Cook for 1–2 minutes until set and pulling away from the sides. Gently flip and cook for an additional 1–2 minutes. Repeat to make 12 crêpes in total.

4 To serve, roll or fold the crêpes, drizzle with the apricot sauce, and sprinkle the toasted hazelnuts and coconut on top.

Nutrition per crêpe	
Calories	130
Total Fat	5g
Saturated Fat	2g
Cholesterol	30mg
Sodium	25mg
Total Carbohydrate	25g
Dietary Fibre	4g
Sugars	10g
Protein	4g

Why not try...

Instead of hazelnuts, garnish with the same amount of toasted almonds.

CRANBERRY PISTACHIO BISCOTTI

Italian-style biscotti have a two-step baking process. Here they're wonderfully textured with chewy cranberries and crunchy pistachios. Enjoy as a treat with coffee or tea.

MAKES 12 · PREP 25 MINS · COOK 1 HR 20 MINS

175g (6oz) chickpea flour

1 tsp baking powder

60g (2oz) coconut oil, slightly warmed

150g (5½oz) sugar

2 tsp vanilla extract

2 large eggs

zest of 1 large orange

pinch of ground nutmeg

75g (2½oz) dried cranberries

85g (3oz) coarsely chopped unsalted pistachios

1 Preheat the oven to 150°C (300°F). Line a baking tray with baking parchment. In a large mixing bowl combine the chickpea flour and baking powder.

2 In a medium mixing bowl whisk together the coconut oil, sugar, vanilla, eggs, orange zest, and nutmeg. In the large mixing bowl, fold the oil-sugar mixture into the flour mixture until incorporated. Gently stir in the cranberries and pistachios until just incorporated.

3 Transfer the mixture to the baking tray and form into a flat, rectangular loaf, about 3cm (1in) high. Bake for 35 minutes, or until lightly brown and set through the centre. Leave to cool for 15–20 minutes.

4 Transfer the baking parchment to a flat work surface. Cut the loaf into 12 equal strips. Transfer the parchment back to the baking tray. Flip the strips onto their cut sides, and evenly space out on the tray. Bake again for 20 minutes, or until firm and light golden brown. Let cool completely before serving, or store in an airtight container in the fridge for 2–3 days.

Nutrition per cookie	
Calories	180
Total Fat	7g
Saturated Fat	4.5g
Cholesterol	30mg
Sodium	20mg
Total Carbohydrate	25g
Dietary Fibre	2g
Sugars	17g
Protein	4g

Why not try...

Use an equal amount of almond extract and chopped almonds instead of the vanilla and pistachios.

CHICKPEA & PEANUT COOKIES

These cookies have the nutritional boost of chickpeas, plus they're naturally gluten-free.

MAKES 20 · PREP 45 MINS · COOK 15 MINS

125g (4½oz) cooked chickpeas

250g (9oz) smooth peanut butter

1 large egg, lightly beaten

1 tsp vanilla extract

100g (3½oz) sugar

¾ tbsp agave nectar

1 Preheat the oven to 180°C (350°F). In a food processor, pulse the chickpeas until they are the consistency of coarse ground almonds. Transfer to a medium mixing bowl.

2 Add the peanut butter, egg, vanilla, sugar, and agave. Stir to combine. Refrigerate for 30 minutes.

3 Line a baking sheet with baking parchment. Take 1 tablespoon of the mixture, roll into a ball, and place on the sheet. Repeat to use all the mixture. With a spatula, flatten the balls.

4 Bake the cookies for 7 minutes, then rotate the sheet 180 degrees and bake for another 7–8 minutes until set and light golden brown. Let cool to room temperature before removing from the baking sheet. Store in an airtight container for up to 2 days.

Nutrition per cookie

Calories	80
Total Fat	3.5g
Saturated Fat	1g
Cholesterol	10mg
Sodium	5mg
Total Carbohydrate	9g
Dietary Fibre	1g
Sugars	7g
Protein	3g

● **Make it vegan**

Substitute 1 ripe mashed banana for the egg.

THREE CITRUS POLENTA CAKE

This not-too-sweet cake blends the zingy flavours of lemon, orange, and grapefruit.

SERVES 10 · PREP 30 MINS · COOK 45 MINS

60ml (2fl oz) fluid coconut oil

3 large eggs

zest and juice of 1 lemon, about 4½ tsp juice

zest and juice of 1 orange, about 80ml (2¾fl oz) juice

zest and juice of 1 grapefruit, about 120ml (4fl oz) juice

200g (7oz) polenta

75g (2½oz) chickpea flour

1¼ tsp baking powder

100g (3½oz) granulated sugar

30g (1oz) icing sugar

1 Preheat the oven to 180°C (350°F). In a small mixing bowl whisk together the coconut oil, eggs, lemon zest and juice, orange zest and juice, and grapefruit zest and juice.

2 In a large mixing bowl, whisk together the polenta, chickpea flour, baking powder, and sugar. Fold in the fruit mixture until just combined.

3 Pour the mixture into a greased 20cm (8in) springform or loose-bottomed cake tin. Place the tin on a baking sheet and bake for 30–35 minutes until set and a skewer inserted into the centre comes out clean. Let rest in the tin for 10 minutes before removing the sides. Dust with icing sugar and serve.

Nutrition per serving

Calories	210
Total Fat	8g
Saturated Fat	5g
Cholesterol	55mg
Sodium	30mg
Total Carbohydrate	32g
Dietary Fibre	2g
Sugars	16g
Protein	5g

● **Make it vegan**

Instead of the eggs, use 3 tablespoons ground flax seeds mixed with 9 tablespoons water.

BERRY & LIME MUNG BEAN ICE POPS

Refreshingly tart and naturally sweet, these lollies are the perfect low-calorie treat for a hot day.

MAKES 10 · PREP 20 MINS, PLUS 6 HRS TO FREEZE

225g (8oz) blueberries
225g (8oz) blackberries
60g (2oz) cooked mung beans
3 tbsp lime juice
80ml (2½fl oz) agave nectar
80ml (2½fl oz) water

1 In a blender or food processor, purée the blueberries, blackberries, mung beans, lime juice, agave, and water until completely smooth.

2 Pour the mixture through a fine sieve to remove the seeds. Press the mixture against the sieve to retain as much liquid as possible.

3 Pour the liquid into 10 lollipop moulds. Insert a stick into each mould. Freeze for at least 6 hours or overnight before serving.

Pulse exchange

Use 150g (5oz) cooked **moth beans** instead of the mung beans.

Nutrition per pop	
Calories	45
Total Fat	0g
Saturated Fat	0g
Cholesterol	0mg
Sodium	0mg
Total Carbohydrate	11g
Dietary Fibre	2g
Sugars	7g
Protein	1g

INDEX

Entries in **bold** indicate ingredients.